*I have written this book,*
*LOVE IS THE GREATEST,*
*in honor of*
*The Lord Jesus Christ who*
*perfectly emulates love.*

Dr. Donald H. Sautter

# LOVE *is the* GREATEST

*A Commentary on First Corinthians 13:1-13*

**LOVE IS THE GREATEST**


Stratton Press Publishing
831 N Tatnall Street Suite M #188,
Wilmington, DE 19801
www.stratton-press.com
1-888-323-7009



ISBN (Paperback): 978-1-64895-149-7
ISBN (Ebook): 978-1-64895-150-3

Printed in the United States of America

# CONTENTS

# DEDICATED
# TO
# MY CHILDREN AND
# THEIR CHILDREN:

Deborah Ann Zakarian
Karina
Klara

Donald Grey Sautter
Natasha
Katie

Donna Esther Mann
Brendan
Liam

# READER ENDORSEMENTS

*"Love is the Greatest uses the language of theology and the best-known letter of St. Paul to relate this universal value of love to our current world. Dr. Sautter points out how divisive attitudes and behaviors draw one away from harmony and empathy that are so necessary in this complex, modern world. Using the example of the life of Jesus, as well as the self- sacrifice of St. Paul, Dr. Sautter paints a clear picture of the ideal."*

*Paul Giella, PhD*

*"Dr. Sautter has written a masterpiece to remind us all of what truly is the most important thing in life which is Love. I recommend this book to everyone to assist them in their journey of Love."*

*Mr. Chris Godwin*

*"I could not read a page without stopping often to contemplate what I had just read. To be sure, it was truly a learning experience. I guarantee that you will think, feel and act differently because this book will change your life."*

*Jean D. Thomas*

# ACKNOWLEDGEMENTS

Donald G. Sautter "Don"- My beloved son who has faithfully been like a "best friend."

Don Christensen- My special friend for his godly counsel, faithfulness, and generosity.

Helen Leflar "Mom"- Who modeled love to me.

Paul Giella, PhD. - My psychologist whose insights have inspired me.

Lauren McElhiney- My assistant, typist and editor for her faithful work night and day to make this book possible.

Pastor Karen- Whose unconditional love and biblically ecumenical ministry has meant so much to me.

Peter Raftery- Who has faithfully been a particularly good friend and consistent model of the Lord Jesus Christ to me.

# PREFACE

***LOVE IS THE GREATEST*** is probably the most unique book on love that has ever been written. This is because of the Apostle Paul's literary style.

It begins with his portrayal of love in relation to: (1) the tongues of men and Angels;(2) The gift of prophecy;(3) Faith that moves mountains;(4) Martyrdom; (see verses 13:1-3).

Then it proceeds to the 17 elements of love (see verses 13: 4-13). The comparisons and contrasts of these verses are incomparable to any description of love. Hence, since this book is not a novel, it should not be read like one. Rather it should be read in short intervals. Note that **LOVE IS THE GREATEST** is a commentary and therefore it should be read like one. That way, you, the reader will best digest the overall context of the book.

# INTRODUCTION

Here is another exposition on love: why? First, because there are very few books that give substantial devotion to the subject. By substantial, I mean books that are based upon the Bible, which alone portrays the pure essence of love.

Yes, I am well aware of Henry Drummond's "The Greatest Thing in the World," Granville T. Walker's, "The Greatest of These," Eileen Guder's "To Live in Love," and I highly recommend them to you. I am also well aware of the many commentaries on 1 Corinthians that relate to the chapter on love. Yet, at the same time, having studied just about every solid commentary on this book, I was amazed to find how little space was given to the thirteenth chapter.

So, although there are other books and commentaries on this subject, I believe the greatest subject in the world deserves many more books. Surely, if we accept as the truth the words of the saying, "What the world needs now is love," then whatever books we can write to encourage love will not be in vain.

Furthermore, in addition to the above objective reason for another book on love, I also have several subjective reasons growing out of my own life that has changed through the love of God.

With the hope that some of the events from my life will open your heart and mind to read this book, I would like to share with you how love has changed me. The people who have been the greatest help to me suffered from the same problem themselves but found a solution and shared their discovery with me. So that is my motive: to help you the same way someone helped me.

You see, by nature, I am a very unloving person due in part to my upbringing. I was raised in a very unloving environment. In my home, there was much tension, strife, frustration, and division. Because of the lack of love in my home, one by one the members of my family split. Dad left home when I was eight, my older sister left home when I was twelve. When I was fourteen, my older brother left home two months before he graduated from high school to go into the army. Even my younger sister left home when I was twenty-two to get married one month after she graduated from high school.

Why not leave? There was little holding them there. Then why did I stay until I was twenty-five when I married? Because God was teaching me how to love in that environment. I also saw and deeply appreciated the good points of my loyal mother who, regardless of her faults, lovingly poured her life as a living sacrifice into her children so that, unlike her, we wouldn't be raised in an orphanage or foster home.

Another facet of my life that related to the theme of this book is my education. Probably the biggest reason why I went to college and graduate school for twelve years full-time was insecurity. Yes, I had different reasons then, but I was not conscious of the real reason. For instance, I went to the Philadelphia College of Bible for my Bachelor of Science degree because I wanted to learn the Bible. I went to the Reformed Episcopal Seminary for my Bachelor of Divinity degree because I wanted to systematize my Bible knowledge into a theological framework. I went to Westminster Theological Seminary for my master's degree in apologetics because I wanted a broad perspective of philosophy and non-Christian theology. Along the way, I went to Ohio State University and the Community College of Philadelphia to learn German and French because I wanted a broader outlook on the arts and sciences of the world. Lastly, I went to Dallas Theological Seminary for my doctorate in the Greek New Testament and exegesis because I wanted to complete all of my studies on the basis of the original languages of the Bible (Hebrew and Greek), so I could be an expert in the original sources of the Hebrew culture and Christian faith.

Nevertheless, underlying all these conscious reasons was an unconscious one, my insecurity. This hit me suddenly when a group of professors at Dallas told me that after I completed my doctoral residence work and before I finished my dissertation, I should get into the ministry and prove myself. They had serious questions about how much my twelve years of full-time education had helped me where it counts in the heart, not the head. I'm also writing this book partly as an outgrowth of my success in business. During my last seven years of graduate schools, I worked as a salesman and manager for the Southwestern Company of Nashville, Tennessee. I had two conscious reasons for doing this: 1) to develop myself practically for the ministry by selling books door-to-door in over ten thousand homes and teaching other students to do the same; 2) to support myself through all these years of school without going into debt. By God's grace, I accomplished those two goals, but it was not until later that I found out the underlying, unconscious reason why I went into sales: insecurity. I was an unloving person, and deep down inside of me I knew it. So, I tried to solve the problem by positive thinking programs and selling techniques, all of which I later found were inadequate in themselves to develop me in love, although I still gained much from them. Even though I was the number 1 salesman for three consecutive years, number 1 student manager of the Bible Library Division for five consecutive years, and even number 1 organizational manager in the whole company, ahead of more than five thousand men from colleges all over the country, from Harvard and Yale to Dallas Seminary and UCLA, still I was insecure. Despite the tens of thousands of dollars that I made in that job over those seven summers, I still was insecure!

But what really shocked me was my first year in the ministry. There are many ministers who refer to the first year of ministry as the "honeymoon year." Man! That was not true for me at all. It was my worst year. There I was, beginning my lifetime of ministry, attempting to blend together my twelve years of education and my seven years of selling and managing into a dynamic ministry. As I started in the fall of 1970 in Valley Forge, I felt confident that I had so much to offer. My attitude surely came across as "you people in Valley Forge are very privileged to have me." What a shame.

From October 1970 to June 1978, the church grew from nothing to about seventy people. However, I was blindly unaware of the trail of offenses, mistakes, and blunders that I was leaving behind me. But in the first week of June, they caught up with me and clobbered me in the head. Seven families left the church. They said I was egotistical, arrogant, cocky, and unloving. Oh, how right they were.

It was then that I began to understand 1 Corinthians 13. How I could enter into those first three verses of the chapter! "If I speak with the tongues of men and of angels, but do not have love, I have become a noisy gong or a clanging cymbal." I must confess that is what I was. In spite of my study of languages, Greek for eleven years, Hebrew for nine years, German for five years, and French for three years, I sounded like a noisy gong!

Then I began to understand verse 2: "And if I have the gift of prophecy, and know all mysteries and all knowledge, and if I have all faith as to move mountains, but do not have love, I am nothing." I discovered that in spite of my ability to preach and teach and even motivate people, in spite of my twelve years of higher education and the resultant degrees, in spite of my self-confidence that was developed during seven years of success in the dog-eat-dog business world, I was nothing, a big zero!

Likewise. I carne to understand verse three: "And if I give all my possessions to feed the poor, and if I deliver my body to be burned, but do not have love, it profits me nothing." In spite of my leaving the prosperity of the business world, in spite of giving away all of our earnings to various charitable institutions, in spite of being willing to die as a martyr for Christ, I still agonizingly discovered that it profited me nothing. What a hard truth to swallow! But I did accept it.

Is it any wonder, then, that since June 1971, I have devoted myself to a pursuit of love? Is it any wonder that I would be more consumed with this pursuit than with any other? My very own life, meaningfulness in life, usefulness in the ministry, and sense of fulfillment to justify my existence in this world were at stake. Is it any wonder that I would write this book to share with you something that I have learned in love, so that you, too, can be kept from a life of waste?

The pure motive and earnest prayer behind this book are to serve you, the reader, with some insights into the greatest thing in this world, and the only thing that we shall carry with us into the next.

In the words of Browning, I implore you to learn love: "For life with all it yields of joy and woe and hope and fear, is just our chance o' the prize of learning love-how love might be, hath been indeed, and is."

# PART 1

## *God's Explanation of Love*

The book *In His Steps*, written by Charles M. Sheldon, challenges the Christian to visualize himself in the footsteps of Christ. The author exposes what many Christians really are compared to what they ought to be. From this standpoint, the book is hardly an enjoyable one. However, for the Christian who is really sincere about being his best for God, it is a welcomed challenge.

Unfortunately, such a spirit of openness to a candid presentation of truth is not too common. For instance, what if Jesus were to visit your church this Sunday? Would He really be welcome?

In essence, of course, Jesus is everywhere by means of His spiritual presence, but what I mean is, is He welcome at your church in a personal way. Would your church feel comfortable in His presence? Would you?

Many people would have to say no in answer to these questions. I suppose there are many reasons for this, but one in particular is that they do not understand the nature of the love of God in Christ.

Therefore, in part 1, we plan to introduce you to the love of God in Christ as portrayed in 1 Corinthians 13. In verses 1 to 3 we are going to see the necessity of love; in verses 4 to 7, the functions of love; in verses 8 to 13, the permanence of love.

First Corinthians 13 is one of the greatest chapters of the Bible. Adolf Harnack says it is "the greatest, strongest, and deepest thing Paul ever wrote." Other authorities acclaim that although Plato did a great work on lone in his *Symposium*, AD 107, Paul in 1 Corinthians 13 has surpassed him and all other writers on the subject. So let us see what he has to say.

## I. The Necessity of Love (Vv. 1–3)

In the opening paragraph, Paul sets forth the necessity of love by comparing *love* to spiritual gifts. His point is that love is more important than any, or all of the most coveted gifts.

### *A. More than the Gift of Tongues*

In verse 1, he specifically singles out the gift of tongues. It is interesting that although Paul apparently recognized the gift of tongues as the least of gifts, he mentions it first. The reason is that the Corinthian believers were so immature in their Christian experience that they considered tongues to be just the opposite, the greatest gift. So Paul begins at their point of need and pierces through their false notion by stressing that without love, their speaking of all the foreign languages in the world made them at best like noisy gongs. They were perhaps something like Cleopatra.

Cleopatra was a great linguist. She could speak the languages of the Ethiopian, Hebrew, Arabic, Syrian, Median, and Parthian ambassadors, says Plutarch. She could turn her tongue to whatever dialect she pleased. But without the *love* of God even she was nothing.

### *B. More than the Gift of Prophecy*

Paul moves from the gift of tongues to the greatest gifts. He shows that love is more important than the gifts of prophecy and faith. His point is that even if one could know all the deep counsels of God (mysteries) and possess all knowledge, and if one even had faith to move mountains, without *love*, he would be nothing. That is, he is nobody, nothing, zero.

### *C. More than Charity and Martyrdom*

Paul continues the same line of logic, comparing love to the sacrifices of one's possessions and life itself. He mentions giving up of goods and the body, but not the soul. The reason is that the soul is the sphere of love. Although the sacrifice of goods may be commendable, without love, it profits one nothing. Likewise, even giving up one's body in martyrdom—without love—profits nothing at all. In the time of the Roman emperor Diocletian, some of the early Christians actually courted martyrdom. How foolish without love! Some think Paul's reference here could be to an Indian, Zarmano-chegas, who burned himself in public on a funeral pyre and had the inscription say that he was immortal. But without love, this act helped him not at all.

Paul's key emphasis in this first paragraph is that our gifts and deeds, no matter how great, are worthless unless we use them in a loving way. Next, in verses 4 to 7, he shows "the way, the truth, and the life" of love as personified in the Lord Jesus Christ (cf. John 14:6).

## II. The Nature Functions of Love (Vv. 4–7)

In this paragraph, Paul portrays the functions, or conduct, of love in a marvelous rhapsody. Love here is seen as a person, and that person is none other than Jesus Christ the Lord. The Greek word *agape* (love) reflects the nature of love as a beautiful, steady, flowing stream. But that picture is not adequate; the portrayal is only fulfilled in Jesus.

So we are going to visualize ourselves going through an art museum where there are fifteen portraits of the life of Christ. We are going to pause for a moment at each one to admire the beauty of the love of God in Christ.

### *A. Love Is Patient*

In the first portrait, we see the title "Love Is Patient." This portrait depicts Christ weeping with deep longing, anguish, and passion over the people of Jerusalem. "Oh Jerusalem, Jerusalem! How often I wanted to gather your children together, just as a hen gathers her brood under her wings, and you would not have it!" (Luke 13:34). Here we see that love is patient because Jesus was patient with the capital city of Israel. How long He waited so patiently for Jerusalem to repent, but her people would not. What unbelief on the part of Israel, but what love on the part of Christ!

### *B. Love Is Kind*

The second portrait is entitled "Love Is Kind." We see Jesus with children gathered around Him, sitting on His lap. "Let the children alone, and do not hinder them from coming to me, for the kingdom of heaven belongs to such as these." (Matt. 19:14).

His kindness was seen in His compassion not only for children but also for the despised, the outcast, and the downtrodden.

*C. Love Is Not Jealous*

The next portrait presents Christ speaking with the rich young ruler. His features strikingly indicate that He is not jealous of the young man's worldly goods. All we see is genuine concern for the young ruler's side. That is true love.

D. Love Does Not Brag

In the next picture, Jesus is being pressured by the Pharisee having done great miracles by the power of the Spirit, Jesus was asked about the source of His power. He answered, "The Son can do nothing of Himself, unless it is something He sees His Father doing; for whatever the Father does, these things the Son also does in like manner" (John 5:19). Love does not brag, and neither did Jesus.

*E. Love Is Not Arrogant*

We see Jesus now in the Garden of Gethsemane, praying on His knees. He wrestles with the will of God the night before His crucifixion. The devil tries to put Him to death there in seclusion. It looks like Satan will be successful because Jesus is sweating drops of blood. In His humanity, Jesus cannot understand it. He cries aloud, "Father, if Thou art willing remove this cup from me; yet not my will, but Thine be done" (Luke 22:42). Even in the face of death in what appeared to be the wrong place, in the garden instead of the cross, Jesus was willing to submit to the will of God. Why? Because love is not arrogant, and neither was Christ.

*F. Love Does Not Act Unbecomingly*

Now we behold Jesus in a debate with the Pharisees. They are trying to trap Him, trying to trick Him, doing their best to get something on Him. But no matter what they think, say, or do, Jesus does not act unbecomingly because love does not.

*G. Love Does Not Seek Its Own*

This is a picture of Jesus suffering from great loss of sleep. He has given Himself to others all day, but instead of going to sleep, He goes into the woods, kneels down, and prays all night. Why did He do this? Because love does not seek its own.

*H. Love Is Not Provoked*

In the next hallway, as we turn the corner, the first picture on our left is of Jesus with His twelve disciples near the end of His ministry. The disciples look perplexed, confused, and frustrated because they still do not understand Him. But is Jesus upset? No, He is not provoked.

True, He does say, "Have I been so long with you, and yet you have come to know me?" (John 14:9). Yet this was an expression of grief and earnestness, for love is not provoked at all.

*I. Love Does Not Take into Account a Wrong Suffered*

This picture is difficult to fully appreciate because it is of Jesus being betrayed by Judas. In spite of such a low blow, Jesus is not angered. He accepts the whole matter with serenity and peace that surpasses all human understanding. Love does not take into account a wrong suffered, even the wrong of a betrayal.

*J. Love Does Not Rejoice in Unrighteousness*

We are moving forward to Calvary, and on the way we see a portrait of Christ at this unfair trial before the Sanhedrin. However, instead of being alarmed about the possibility of His innocence being mistaken for guilt, Jesus is rather grieved over the unrighteousness of His accusers. Jesus cared for them, and yet at the same time He was grieved because of their unrighteousness. He knew God was working out His will through their unrighteousness.

*K. Love Rejoices in the Truth*

Now we see Jesus hanging on the cross, with the words above His head "King of the Jews." The words were placed there by an ungodly man. They were ridiculed by the crowd. But yet Jesus could rejoice in the truth of them, although dying a criminal's death He did not deserve. Why? Because love rejoices in the truth.

*L. Love Bears All Things*

As He hung on the cross, Jesus cried out to God, "Father, forgive them for they do not know what they are doing" (Luke 23:34). Oh, to what lengths love can go! As He bore the sins of the world, He paused for a moment to show His concern for His mother, saying, "Woman, behold your Son." (John 19:26). With His dying breath, He saw to His mother's welfare, for love bears all things.

*M. Love Believes All Things*

In this picture, Jesus turns to John, His beloved disciple, and says, "Behold your mother. And from that hour the disciple took her into his own household" (John 19:27). He believed in John, but He also believed in the other disciples whom John symbolically represented. He believed in their potential, although they had forsaken and fled from the cross, for love believes all things.

*N. Love Hopes All Things*

At the end, Jesus cried out, "It is finished!" By these words, He confessed that He hoped in the eternal value of His mission. He did not despair, for He hoped and knew that His death accomplished the redemption of all who believe. His death was satisfactory completion of His life's work because love hopes all things.

*O. Love Endures All Things*

We gaze upon Jesus in this last picture as He walks down the road to Emmaus with two disciples. He expounds the Word of God to them from the Old Testament scriptures. He warms their hearts by His abiding ministry. He had endured all things with His triumph over the grave. Love endures forever. Why? Because love endures all things.

**III. The Permanence of Love**

Actually, there are seventeen characteristics of love in verses 4 to 13, if we include "love never fails" and "love is the greatest." In the following chapters, all seventeen characteristics shall be treated separately. But here we shall consider these last two characteristics in contrast to the gifts and in connection with perfection.

*A. In Contrast to the Gifts*

This third and last paragraph of 1 Corinthians 13 begins with the words "Love never fails." This is a new term for the perpetuity of love. Here love is seen as surviving everything. Love is never to be out of use. Love always holds its peace. Love even outlasts those three greatly appreciated gifts of prophecy, tongues, and knowledge. Paul's perspective on all these things is that whereas the greatest and the least gifts of man will fail, love will not.

*B. In Connection with Perfection*

It is difficult to know for sure what the word *perfect* means. Some think it refers to the completed canon of scripture. I cannot agree with that because the idea seems so foreign to the context. Others think it means Christ's Second Coming. This is a good possibility. Still others believe that it refers to that realm of reality that God will set up in the future after Christ's return. I lean toward this last view.

When such perfection comes, especially in the new heavens and the new earth in which righteousness shall dwell, the partial things shall be done away; immaturity, childishness, and ignorance shall be gone, having given way to maturity, vision, and understanding. The enduring qualities of faith, hope, and love will abide, but even among these three, love is the greatest. This is the love of God in Christ. This can also be the love of God in you, as you acquaint yourself with it in the succeeding chapters of this book.

No wonder the immortal words of the great martyr Elizabeth Folks live on. She said her last words at the stake. "Farewell, faith; farewell, hope." And taking the stake in hand, she exclaimed, "Welcome, love!"

# PART 2

## *God's Explanation of Love*

# LIFE MESSAGE 1

## *Love Is Patient*

If you have ever watched a beam of light striking a prism, then you know the experience of seeing the different rays of color: red, orange, yellow, green, blue, indigo, and violet—all the colors of the solar spectrum. It's truly a sight to behold. One beam of light, but many rays of color.

That is the way we can best approach 1 Corinthians 13:4–13. For as Granville Walker says, "The Holy Spirit used the inspired intellect of the Apostle Paul as a prism through which he radiated the beam of light of love and had it come out the other side in all its rays of color."

As we look at the first color, we see that love is patient. Patience is one of seventeen rays of color of the most magnificent force of all the world, the force of love. Now we have to take that one ray of color and send it through another prism to understand something of what it is all about. What is meant by "love is patient"? We want to answer that question in three ways: by looking at patience in attitude, in words, and in actions.

## I. Patience in Attitude

To get the force of Paul's meaning, we should translate his description "Love bears patience, or love produces patience." This must first take place in the realm of the attitude, the realm of the subconscious as well as the conscious within us, the inner man, that which we call heart. This is where patience begins. As Proverbs 23:7 puts it, "For as he (the man) thinks within himself, so he is." Or as the riddle goes, "You are not what you think you are, but you *think*, you are." What you are thinking, that is what you really are.

### *A. The Basis of Patience*

If a person is going to build a life of patience, he must have a foundation. The foundation of our attitude of patience must be the fact that God is God. For instance, Paul had this foundation when he described his ministry at Corinth. He said that although he planted and Apollos watered, God gave the increase. God made the church grow.

If I have as the basis of my attitude a recognition that God is God, that all that happens God causes, and that all He wants for me is good and for His glory, and if I trust Him regardless of what comes across my path, I can be patient because I'm letting God be God. That's the attitude of patience.

### *B. The Definition of Patience*

Paul did not write long definitions. He did not create a dictionary of terms, but rather he described what love produces. When he said that love produces patience, or perhaps more literally, love suffers long, he meant that quality in a person that knows no limit to restfulness in the fact that God is God. Patience is the attitude that says, no matter what comes, "I will not get ruffled because I know that this is for my good and for God's glory." Regardless of what happens, whatever touches a believer, he must do right, not wrong, in the face of it. He must think right in the face of it, regardless. Even if this means suffering l-o-n-g. He must be patient rather than become angry, impetuous, hasty, and later regret what he forfeited of his character in Christ in the face of a trial.

### *C. The Confidence of Patience*

Perhaps the best way to describe the confidence of patience is to tell you about the Trail Ridge Road in the Rocky Mountains of Colorado. This is called the highest road in the world through mountain ranges. On this road, you almost become lost in a world of mountain peaks, but when you come to Longs Peak, you enter a problem area. That problem happens to be fog, or clouds, so that you can't see anything ahead of you, hardly even the road itself. All you can hope for is that as you drive very slowly, soon the clouds will lift. Of course, you drive with the confidence that the road is there and that the mountain tops are all around, even though for the moment you cannot see them. But they are there, then suddenly the clouds lift, not by your power, either. You did nothing to move those clouds. They just lift and you say, "Oh, how beautiful! How beautiful!" That helps us to understand the confidence of patience.

Who hasn't gone through some clouds of circumstance, clouds you cannot control? All you know is that the road is there; the most you can do is take one step at a time, step by step, and pray and hope that God will lift the clouds. That's the confidence of patience.

In our local prayer meetings, we have asked God to make His power known in our church, that He would raise up a mighty church for Himself, that He would so do such great work through our ministry that the world would have to say, "God did it." Sometimes it's hard to come back week after week and not see all the things we want to see in the lives of people and in the growth of the work. But perhaps far more important than God giving us numbers is God giving us patience. God sends the clouds for a period of time because love and patience are far more important to Him than a packed church building. Our attitude is all-important; we think not just in terms of the church, but in terms of our own lives. The question, therefore, comes: Are you willing to be patient as a Christian? If so, suffer long. Remember, winners never quit and quitters never win. Remember, hasty action never promotes the purposes of God. And remember that if you don't suffer long with love, you'll probably wind up suffering in other areas anyhow.

## II. Patience in Word

Next we come to patience in word. This is our response to how life affects us. Threatening circumstances often expose what a person is really like inside. Hear the words of an individual in response to a threatening situation, and you have a revelation of what that person is really like.

These kinds of situations often occur in the church among God's people. We regret the impatient words we speak. Before we speak hastily, we must suffer long. If we don't, we shall suffer after we have said those words, in a different way. The quality of long suffering must condition what we say. If a brother offends us, dare we slash back and retaliate?

Let's leave the church scene and go to the home. Does your wife, your husband, or your children do things that threaten you and your own estimate of yourself? Do you, as a result, slash back with your words? Do you say something that you ought not to say because you do not suffer long in the face of those circumstances? These situations are involved in patience in word.

The basic rule is this: whatever happens to you, your words should never reflect impatience. If they do, you are not acting in a loving way to yourself, to God, to your loved ones, or to others. Again, let that quality of suffering long condition your words as well as your attitude.

May I encourage you to read the Psalms. The Psalms over and over again admonish us to stop hasty action, hasty words, and hasty thoughts and to wait upon the Lord. Oh, but waiting is so hard to do! That's why God says love suffers long. Wait, yes; suffer long, but wait patiently.

### III. Patience in Action

This refers to our relationship to our fellow men, especially to three different kinds of our fellow men.

#### *A. Toward Difficult People*

Do you know any people who are hard to get along with—besides yourself, I mean? What should be your action toward them according to the Bible, not according to your own thoughts, not according to even the mixture of the thoughts you had before you were saved and the ones that you presently have now that you are saved, but according to the Word of God purely? Should you rid yourself of them as the Pharisees did with their "holier than thou" attitude? Should you split from somebody because you can't get along with him? Is that really what God says? No! Your conscience as well as the Holy Spirit, I'm sure, convinces you that that is not the way. So much of the New Testament, even this very chapter, aims at keeping believers together, not making them split apart. But what do you do about a difficult person? Let me teach you by way of contrast.

The Greeks taught different kinds of virtues, but patience was not among them. As a matter of fact, Aristotle said that one of the greatest virtues was the strength of a man to retaliate when he was wronged, even to the point of death. This is where you get the idea of having a duel when a man had said something wrong to you.

But by contrast, the Lord Jesus Christ says virtue is having somebody hurt you, even seventy times seven, and then refuse to retaliate. Why? Because God is God. I know Christians I can't even hurt once without their slapping me back in the face, so to speak. But the truth is, love suffers long, even toward different people.

*B. Toward Impossible People*

Let me illustrate with a story. Robert G. Ingersoll, the brilliant atheist of the nineteenth century, in the midst of one of his profound lectures said all kinds of things against God and then added, "I will give God five minutes to strike me down dead for all things I have said against Him." For five minutes, he arrogantly waited for God to strike him down. The five minutes passed, and he went on with a smile and a smirk of satisfaction.

When Theodore Parker, the great man of God of the day, heard about it, he said, "Did the man really believe he could exhaust the patience of the eternal God in five minutes?"

Our actions toward even the impossible people, who would think and perhaps say all kinds of things against us should be, after five minutes, patient like the eternal God.

### *C. Toward Nice People*

What about nice people like your wife, your husband, your parents, and all the ones you call your loved ones? I personally find that the ones with whom I am most impatient are the ones whom I love the most. It is not the impossible person. It is not the difficult person. It is the one I love the most, especially God. I am not pleased about the fact that God is not doing what I want fast enough. And, of course, right down the line with my wife and children.

Love suffers long. Love takes daily count of what you must do to your loved ones, especially in being one who bears patience. If you bear patience toward the ones you love the most, you will have no problem dealing with anybody else.

I have to conclude, therefore, when someone is impatient toward me, it is because he is impatient toward God.

## Application

How can you begin a new and fresh today being a patient Christian? It's as simple as your ABCs. Look at James 1:2–3: "Consider it all joy (consider, that's attitude) my brother, when you encounter various trials, knowing that the testing of your faith produces endurance." In the King James Version, it says "patience," but a more accurate word is *endurance*. Endurance is patience stretched over a lifetime, patience stretched out.

The way you get patience, in simple terms, is "Be joyous in every trial." Let no trial ruffle you in thought, word, or action. Rejoice before God say, "Thank you, Lord." Be happy in it, even if somebody calls you a bad name, even if they hurt you in some way, even when you get setback financially. Whatever it is, say, "Thank you, Lord." Rejoice in it and say, "Thank you because you have sent this trial to teach me patience if nothing else." That's how to get it.

# LIFE MESSAGE 2

## *Love Is Kind*

Perhaps you know the old fable about the wind and the sun. The wind and the sun debated back and forth about which of them could first cause a man to take off his coat. The wind tried first; it blew, it stormed, and it raged, but the more it did, the tighter the man held his coat. Finally, the wind stopped and in despair let the sun have a try. The sun radiated its warmth on the man. It was not long before the man loosened and took off his coat.

Each one of us has a choice, whether in our marriages, our homes, our churches, or our communities of using the method of the wind or of the sun. The results will be the very same for us, depending on our choice.

Perhaps you say, "I want to use the method of the sun, but oh, the windy, stormy, blasting treatment I get from other people who take advantage of my warm and kind treatment of them! Do I not have to fight wind with wind, or fire with fire? The answer comes from God's words, "Love is kind." Love offers no exceptions to the rule. Regardless of how others treat you, is it not better to choose the method of the sun?

We need a fresh bath in the "Son-shine". I do not mean the s-u-n shine; I mean the S-o-n shine, from God's Son, the Lord

Jesus Christ. To help us get such a bath, we examine the Apostle Paul's words in 1 Corinthians 13:4.

Paul himself had to learn that love is kind. He was at least forty years of age at the time of his conversion. He was a great hater of God's people and poured out all sorts of windy blasts against the Christians of his day. He especially had to learn this lesson. God only knows how long it really took him. We know that he spent at least three years in Arabia after his conversion, but there were an additional fourteen years after that, silent years, about which we just don't know anything concerning the apostle. So there were at least seventeen years between the apostle's conversion and the time he was able to write these words.

Kind? What does that word really mean? It is a word you rarely hear in our present-day society. Have you ever stopped and asked yourself what really is the definition of *kindness*? What does it really mean? Of course, once you saw what it really meant, did you ever really face honestly the complications that you found involved in being kind? Once you've done that, have you been bold enough to endeavor to apply love that is kind?

## I. The Definition of Kindness

### *A. The Contextual Meaning*

As you look at the definition of kindness, you will notice, first of all, the contextual meaning. Many commentators bring that out in verse 4, "Love is patient, love is kind," you have what is known as a couplet. They say that this couplet actually summarizes the next thirteen ingredients of love in the latter part of 1 Corinthians 13. Therefore, when you look at the other different ingredients of love that it is not jealous, does not brag, is not arrogant, etc., these are all different aspects of either love suffering long or love being kind. Of course, other scholars do not feel that way, but most of them think that at least they go together—love suffers long and is kind.

Why do we make this point? Well, for this reason: It's one thing for a Christian to suffer long. And, of course, some Christian do just that and no more than that, and they sure look like it. Did you ever see the martyr complex? Some believers just sit there enduring. Do you know a Christian who sort of makes you feel like all he is doing is enduring you, suffering long with you? But is it not true that the person who receives such "love" will miss the total impact of a positive manifestation of love? That is why "and is kind" must go along with "love is patient." It is one thing to endure, but it is something else to be kind in the positive sense as well. That is the idea of the contextual meaning of being kind.

*B. The Literal Meaning*

As for the literal meaning, I want to quote John Short as follows:

> The word as used here denotes to be good natured, gentle, tender, affectionate. Love wishes well. Kindness is not harsh, sour, morose or ill-natured; kindness is being courteous. The idea is that under all provocations and ill-usage, kindness is gentle and mild. Hatred prompts one to harshness, severity, unkindness of expression, anger, and a desire for revenge. On the contrary, love is the reverse of all these. A Christian who truly loves someone will be kind, desirous of doing that person good, will be gentle not severe, not harsh, will be courteous not

> morose, because he desires that other person's happiness in all circumstances and would not dare to pain his feelings. Love is constantly kind in this manner.

This description reminds me of those Christians in the first century. They died at the hands of Nero; they were cast into the arena and fed to the lions. What impressed Nero and the Romans of that day was not that the Christians were willing to die for Christ, and even sing as they walked out into the arena, but that they went to death with a smile of kindness on their faces. Over and over again, as he went from one part of the arena to the other, the smiles, kind and gentle smiles on the faces of these Christians. They did not only suffer, and even suffer long unto death, but they were kind to the end as well, kind even in the face of the worst enemy of all: death itself.

But what about the person who turns you off? What about the person who wrongs you? What about the person who is cold to you? What about the person who provokes you? And what about you when you're just plain tired? Are you not justified to be unkind in situations like these? Don't these complications mean anything at all to God?

Doesn't He understand that we're only human?

The answer is that "love is kind" is in the present tense, the durative tense, the tense of continuous action, which sees in it no kind of imperfection or discontinuance of the act. It is something that endures, is constant and ongoing, something that is consistent. Therefore, there are no exceptions.

You see, love is something; love is kind. If we have that love in our hearts, regardless what anyone is to us on the outside, our behavior does not change. To express kindness, our love on the inside must be bigger than that force or influence upon us from the outside. So whether a person turns us off, is cold to us, offends us, or provokes us because of repeated mistakes, the answer always comes back: love is kind!

Kindness is being nice to someone regardless of their treatment of you. Kindness is what flows out of you without any thought of the other person's action. If Christ is in us, and if we let His love, His unconditional love, flow out of us like a stream down a mountainside, no obstacle along the way will be a complication.

I want to ask you before the end of this chapter to renew your commitment to God in this matter of being kind. Maybe it never entered your mind to do so; it never did mine. With all my years of preparing for the ministry, with all my years of serving the Lord, I never thought deeply about what it means to be kind, and to commit myself to that action, but I want to do so, and I hope you will too.

Will you try this for at least one week? Say no unkind word about anybody. Don't talk about their mistakes, don't about their problems, don't mention anything negative about them for a week. I challenge you. Just say only positive things, only kind things, only tender things, only compassionate things, only tender-hearted things for a week. I challenge you to see what kind of a person you will be after one week of this.

## II. The Complications of Kindness

What if she says…? Forget it. What if he says…? Don't retaliate. Just gaze at the following scriptures, realizing that they represent God's will for us:

> James 3:17: "But the wisdom from above is first pure, then peaceable, gentle, reasonable,

> full of mercy and good fruits, unwavering without hypocrisy."
>
> 1 Peter 3:8–9: "To sum up, let all be harmonious, sympathetic, brotherly, kind-hearted, and humble in spirit; not returning evil for evil, or insult for insult, but giving a blessing instead; for you were called for the very purpose that you might inherit a blessing."

Therefore, 1) when someone wrongs you, realize love as kindness acts with goodness toward those who ill-treat it. It is gracious and kind as opposed to malice and ill will. It is one of the softer graces of God.

2) When someone is cold to you, realize kindness is being nice to someone. It is tender and compassionate in itself and does not depend on outward circumstances. It is mild and obliging to others.

3) When someone turns you off, realize love as kindness is full of gentleness and considerateness. It extends good to others. In commenting on Ephesians 4:31, Martin Luther explained it this way, "We should love God so much that we will not purposefully tell lies about anyone, nor mention his mistakes, nor talk concerning him, but we should defend our neighbor and say the best we can about him."

Just think of that! These are the words of the man who remained steadfast in court when asked by the Roman Catholic officials to recant his position that salvation is by faith, who was fearless about standing for the truth, to the point of declaring "Here I stand. God helping me, I can do nothing else, for it would not only be against my conscience, but also against my very sanity, and therefore, I cannot recant and will not."

How we often justify our unkindness by emphasizing that we are only being honest, straightforward, and open. Yet as true as Martin Luther was, he did not allow his stand for truth to negate his responsibility of being kind.

4) When someone doesn't empathize with your tiredness or sickness, realize our Lord Jesus Christ did not mistreat people in return for their mistreatment. He did not let self-pity get the best of Him at a time like that. The Christ-like individual also is one who will accept such a situation as an opportunity to be tested by the Lord, that even in tiredness and sickness he may show you kindness.

## III. The Application of Kindness

You probably raise the question, "Man, this is unreal! This is too far beyond me. I'm human. Yes, I'm a Christian but… surely God doesn't require this of me on this earth now, does He?" We can see from Ephesians 4:32 that he does. Notice what Paul says because he is interested in the application of kindness in our lives, not just its definition in our brains.

### *A. The Goal*

He says, "And be kind." That's in the imperative mood; it's a command. He does not say, "Will you please, if it is at your convenience?" No! He does not say think about it, or pray about it, and then do it. He does not say do it once in a while either. He gives a present command: "Be kind." Be kind all the time because love is kind, not love "was" kind or love "shall be" kind but love "is" kind. Because love is kind, you should be kind because you have God's love in you.

"Be kind to another, tender-hearted, forgiving each other, just as God in Christ also has forgiven you." This verse gives me direction I need. With my choleric temperament, it is not easy for me to be kind. I can become so goal-oriented that I step on people's toes. I can be so full of truth, and tell all kinds of true things, and hurt people's feelings in the process. I speak truth, but I do not do it in love; I do not do it in kindness, and oh, how I hurt people. I have to confess that, but I'm so glad for a verse like this because I find hope in it. Regardless of how people think of me anymore, regardless of what the past has been for me, I have hope because of what this verse says.

I see a goal in this verse.

*B. The Starting Point*

Regardless of the spiritual level you are currently at, you have a goal: to be kind. You may think you are so far from that goal. If you do, that is great because now you have a starting point. After Paul says, "Be kind one to another," he adds, "Be tender-hearted." That's the starting point. How is being tender-hearted a starting point? Simply this: what really motivates you about loving anybody? Begin, for example, with the love of God and keep on telling yourself, "God loves me, God loves me, God loves me." Keep telling yourself this until you begin to believe it and let your heart become tender, anew, and afresh with the love of God.

Why does God love you? Because He sees something good in you?

Because you are handsome or beautiful? Because you are intelligent? Because you are spiritual? Because you are rich or poor? No! He just loves. Oh, how that should make you tender in your heart. Because He loves you like that, and because you are a Christian and a child of God, you can be like Him. You can resemble your Heavenly Father and begin to let that same kind of feeling be communicated to other people. Just *love* them for the sake of loving them, just love people, and let that *love* also have a quality of kindness, just for the sake of kindness. Let it come out of a tender heart because of how God loves you. That is your starting point. Yes, the goal may seem far, but do not worry about that; see the goal and pursue it.

Many times in my past, especially working with salesmen who did not learn quickly enough under my teaching, I would get angry. Spencer Hays, my boss, repeatedly said to me, "Don, you have to be more kind! Be gracious!" Every time he counseled me like that, I would feel mixed emotions. On the one hand, I knew in my heart he was right, but on the other hand, I felt a horrible sense of insecurity. Where do I begin? I did not know where to begin, so I didn't! But you do not have to be at such a loss, for in Ephesians 4:32, I am showing you from my own past experience where to begin. If it works for me, it can work for anybody.

### *C. The Means*

The means by which you can attain that goal of being kind is this:

"Forgiving each other, just as God in Christ also has forgiven you." Many times Christians disobey this command with various excuses: "I'll forgive you, but I won't forget," or "I'll forgive you, but I won't trust you anymore," or "I won't forgive you, I can't forgive you." The question comes, how did Christ forgive? How did God, for Christ's sake, forgive you?

First of all, He did it *freely*. There was no reason why He had to forgive you; you did not earn anything. You did not somehow bribe God to forgive you. He forgave you freely.

Second, He forgave you *completely*. He said, "Not only will I forgive all your sins, but I'll put them behind Me and remember them no more. And as far as the east is from the west, as deep as the deepest ocean, that's how far your sins shall be removed from Me." That's how we should forgive. Have you ever had the experience of being forgiven by somebody, a Christian, and then seeing them later and feeling "Oh, no, he really didn't forgive!"? That is not forgiveness. That is just a diluted, carnal kind of forgiveness. Forgiveness is forgetting also.

If you hold bitterness, and you just cannot forget, God can give you the power. He will help you at least to put it out of your mind each time it comes in. That you can do. You do not have to think on it, and surely you don't have to talk about it.

Third, He forgave *liberally*. He forgave all the many sins we have done. That is the standard by which we should forgive others. This is the means for our growth in kindness. The only thing that complicates our being kind to people is our not forgiving them. If somebody is severe toward you, harsh, morose, or hard, they have not forgiven you. It's that simple. If you forgive them, it flows.

Ian Maclaren, the author of *Beside the Bonnie Brier Bush* and one of the greatest orators of the Christian gospel who ever lived, attempted to preach in his first church without notes. In the midst of his sermon, he would sometimes have to stop and say to the congregation, "Friends, that is not very clear. It was clear in my study on Saturday, but now I will begin again." One day when this happened, a gaunt elder came forward after service, took him by the hand, and said, "When you are not remembering your sermon, my son, just give out a song to us, and we will be singing that while you are taking a rest. Just sit down and rest in that chair, remembering what you were going to say, for we are all loving you and praying for you." With such elders and parishioners, he went on to become a great preacher and a great master of the deep things of the heart. That first church made Ian Maclaren. Years afterward, he said, "I am in the ministry today because of the tenderness and charity of those country folk, those perfect gentlemen and Christians." If *love* is kind, we can experience this same depth of spiritual growth and power in our churches today.

# LIFE MESSAGE 3

## *Love Is Not Jealous*

Oscar Wilde, writing about a trip of Satan through the Libyan Desert, describes a very interesting situation in which Satan was watching his demons tempting a holy hermit. All during this period of time, they were tempting him with sins of the flesh. One by one, the holy hermit victoriously handled each temptation. As time wore on, the devil became more and more impatient. Finally, he went up to his demons and said, "Move aside, let me show you how it's really done." Then he approached the holy hermit and said, "Your brother has just been appointed the monarch of Arabia." The holy hermit responded with a scowl of jealousy, and the victory was the devil's.

### I. Jealousy Causes Hatred toward Others

Would to God that each of us would realize that in God's eyes, the greatest sins are not necessarily the sins of the flesh. Equally great in God's eyes are the sins of disposition, like jealousy. Jealousy is a poison that eats away at the being, character, and personality of the individual and destroys the highest relationship of human beings in life. Unfortunately, we, like the demons, put a higher sense of disapproval on the sins of the flesh. But does not the message of the Spirit come to us afresh to challenge our value system in terms of the gradations of sin?

*A. The Predominance of Jealousy*

Jealousy is near the top of the list. In the apostle's description of love, his first thoughts are about two positive aspects of love. In verse 4, he says that love suffers long and love is kind. But when he describes what love is not, the first thing that comes to his mind is not something to do with sins of the flesh, but with sins of the spirit. "Love is not jealous." That is amazing to me, but it is not new. Think about what happened after Adam and Eve were thrown out of the garden. Their sons, Abel and Cain, were born. Then Cain became jealous of Abel, and because of his jealousy, Cain slew Abel. The first crime committed in all of human history was done out of a premeditation fostered by a feeling of jealousy. In God's book, jealousy heads the list of sins.

Jealousy? What really is jealousy? I want to quote a description from Albert Barnes' *New Testament Notes* that I think is relevant to our understanding of this problem:

> To be jealous or to envy is to feel uneasiness, mortification or disconnect at the sight of superior happiness, excellence or reputation enjoyed by another. To repine at another's prosperity and to fret oneself on account of his real or forced superiority. Of course it may be excited by anything in which another excels or in which he is more favored than are we. It may be its accomplishment, reputation, success; it may extend to any

> employment or rank in life. But one thing is for sure, envy or jealousy lies commonly in the same line of business, occupation and rank. We do not usually envy a monarch, a conqueror, a nobleman unless we are aspiring to the same rank. The farmer does not usually envy the blacksmith, but another farmer. The blacksmith does not usually envy the schoolmaster or the lawyer, but rather another blacksmith. The clergyman does not envy anybody else really, but another clergyman. The physician, another physician; the housewife, another housewife; the businessmen, another businessman and on and on it goes. This is something of what jealousy is all about.

Even kings are disturbed by it! You mean a king would actually be jealous? He has so much, so much power, so many riches, so much of everything. And yet he would be jealous? Yes, and if there was ever a king who should not have been, it was King Saul. He was head and shoulders above all the people in Israel the time. He was God's gift to the nation, so to speak. If there ever was a man who was competent to rule a nation, it was Saul. But one day, he had a seed of jealousy developing in his heart toward a young man called David. That seed of jealousy grew into a root, and that root of jealousy sprouted forth in all sorts of blossoms until it brought about Saul's destruction. His empire fell. He himself fell, and it finally led to death itself. Another man took his place, all because of jealousy.

*B. The Power of Jealousy*

Jealousy is recognized by psychologists, psychiatrists, medical doctors as well as by ministers. It is a vice that grips the disposition of an individual and so keeps him within its clutches that his own good is hindered. Jealousy controls him because of his feelings toward someone else. What a pity! That is jealousy, the power of it, so powerful that it robs people of their joys in life. But where does it come from? What really is the root of the thing?

## II. Jealousy Is Caused by Self-Hatred

What kind of chain reaction really occurs in this process? May I describe to you how it starts? Jealousy is caused by self-hatred. It is not hatred toward others that causes a person to be jealous of another, but self-hatred, me hating myself that causes jealousy toward others. Hatred toward others is the effect—self-hatred is the cause.

*A. The Root of the Problem*

Why would you be jealous of someone anyway? Is it not because you do not really feel fulfilled within yourself for what you are? When you look at yourself from the inside, are you really satisfied? Have you learned to recognize yourself for what you are and to be thankful for it? If you are jealous, it is because you have never accepted how God has made you. You have not learned to rejoice for what you are. Many people do not like the way they look. Many are dissatisfied because their intelligence is not is not as high as they want it to be. Many feel that their skill level in their job is not where they would like it to be. Basically, they suffer from a lack of self-worth. They have not learned to accept themselves. That lack of self-acceptance can be defined as self-hatred.

Harry Emerson Fosdick described it this way. In his psychology of the human personality, he portrayed jealousy as hypersensitivity in someone who has an inferiority complex. It is the expression of a person whose ego is so small and so threatened by other people that it thrashes out in negative feelings, words, and actions. By way of contrast, the superior person—the person who is fulfilled, the person who really accepts himself for what he is, and who has learned to live with and be happy with himself—is described as a banquet for others to attend and eat. But that kind of a banquet is poison to a person with an inferiority complex because it manifests how small he is.

*B. The Chain Reaction*

Self-hatred: how does it progress into hatred for others? Here's how: we really despise what we lack. We have all these inner feelings of inferiority, and then we meet someone who somehow has excelled beyond us in our same rank. We see him, we interact with him a little bit, and our self-hatred causes a feeling of resentment, unthankfulness, lack of appreciation, or jealousy. This jealousy leads to a feeling of bitterness because we are projecting to that person our own lack. We are bitter about the fact that they are what we want to become, and we hate ourselves for not being that. This bitterness grows and grows into hatred for other people. That finally leads to strife and violence. What is the source of quarrels and conflicts among us? "You lust and do not have; so you commit murder" (James 4:2). *Murder*, as referred to here, may be physical murder, but it could also refer to character murder. You will easily find an envious person, a jealous person very, active in character assassination, gossip, and slander. "You hate yourself for what you are not" is what James is saying. You lust to get it, and when you find somebody who has it, you murder them in your thoughts, you are envious and cannot obtain, so you fight and quarrel.

"You do not have because you do not ask," James declares. This reminds me of that gala festival held in Milan, Italy, in honor of the great composer Giuseppe Verdi. Two of the leading composers of the day were invited to present some music in his honor. Toscanini was the one, Mascagni was the other. But interestingly enough, Toscanini had great feelings of envy toward Mascagni. So he said to the management of the festival, "I'll compose anything for Verde that night, in his honor, if you'll pay me more than you'll pay Mascagni." The management thought it over and agreed. The festival went beautifully and after it was over, Toscanini was given one lira. He looked at it with amazement. "What's this?" he demanded. The manager explained to him, "Mascagni did it for free."

Oh, the fools we make of ourselves by being jealous toward someone else. How we reveal how small we really are, how selfish we really are, when we express jealousy. Because the biggest thing we express is how miserable we are inside with self-hatred. Such a power like this can only be cured by love. How so? Well, the opposite of love is hatred. Therefore, the only cure for hatred must be the presence of love. But how can you really cure jealousy in the human heart toward someone else? It has to begin in the human heart?

## III. Jealousy Is Only Cured by Love

Now I want to offer the solution to the problem—and, may I say, it is a universal problem. It is not just Toscanini's;

it is not just Saul's; it is not just mine, but it is yours too. Granville Walker, in his book about jealousy, says he cannot imagine anybody reading his book who does not have a problem with jealousy once in a while; neither can I imagine anybody reading this book who is exempt from the problem of jealousy. Therefore, you should be very much aware of what the cure is. It's the love of God in Christ for you. I know of nothing else that can solve a problem of self-hatred than the love of God. Why? Because of this: We have tried for years to overcome our problems by ourselves. We have tried positive thinking, and that did not work; we have tried getting busy at work and hobbies to get our minds off our problems, and that works only to a certain degree. We have tried all sorts of other things; we have listened to advice and tried to apply it. Even prayer and Bible reading alone are not the answer. What it all comes down to is a personal relationship with a loving God. It begins with the realization that God loves us through Christ, not for what we are not, but if God loves us and accepts us for what we are not, surely we can learn to do that too. As soon as we allow that fact to saturate the very core of our being, we can eliminate self-hatred.

The first and greatest commandment of all is "Thou shalt love the Lord thy God with all thy heart, with all thy soul, with all thy mind and with all thy strength." But we cannot love God without His first loving *us*. John makes that very clear in his epistle, "We love because He first loved us." By ourselves, if we cannot love ourselves or anyone else properly, we cannot love God. But when we receive God's love, then we learn to love Him in return because it is a cause and effect relationship. As soon as we learn to love Him, ascribe worth to Him and praise to Him for who He is, then we have already begun to act the same toward people. That is why the second commandment is like unto it, "Love thy neighbor as thyself." It is only when the love of God in Christ floods the human heart, and makes our hearts feel a sense of acceptance, recognition, security, and stability in God, that we can learn to love ourselves as well as love God. Only when we learn to love ourselves can we love our neighbors. God based His command to love our neighbors on this fact: love your neighbor as yourself. The reason why we are jealous toward people is because we are really jealous toward ourselves. We are really hateful to ourselves. Jealousy is hatred. Jealousy is not love. "Love is not jealous," the Bible says, therefore, hatred must be jealousy, and jealousy must be hatred. So when we are jealous of someone, we are automatically showing hatred. Hatred comes from inside ourselves, from our attitude toward ourselves. When we learn to love God and to feel His love for us, and learn how to love ourselves because of how He loves us, then we can love our neighbors.

Perhaps it can be illustrated like this: Nathaniel Hawthorne should have written about human psychology, but he did not. Yet he did write a book called *The Bosom Serpent*. In it he gave his views on jealousy. It is a story about a man who lost his wife and separated from her because of ill-founded suspicions about her. The suspicions came out of a heart that felt inferior toward itself. He was so gripped by jealousy that it became a serpent in his breast. So gripping was this vice within him, that when he walked down the streets of his town, people asked him, "What's the matter? What's the matter with you? Aren't you feeling well today?" He would say in return, "It gnaws! It gnaws!" That bitter spirit of jealousy was like a serpent gnawing away inside of him, and he looked at everybody through the posture of that jealousy. But one day after he was just about at the end of his rope, his wife came to him again and said, "Honey, why can't you forget yourself and love me?"

Hear her words: forget yourself and love me. With those words, he dropped to the ground, and suddenly there was a sound like the hissing of a snake passing by. It appeared to leap out of his breast, and in a moment, there was ripple in the fountain as it disappeared. When he stood back up again, he forgot himself and loved her.

Beware of that serpent of jealousy in your bosom. Let it pass away. Get rid of it and drown it in the nearest fountain.

Leonardo da Vinci is a great example to us, not only in his paintings, but also in his character. He is known not only for his own work, but also for the way he praised other men. Although he had occasional problems with his enemies, he knew how to praise his friends, especially his fellow craftsmen in the field. In describing one of his friend's paintings of the gates of the temple in Florence, Italy, he called them "Gates of Paradise," thus the coining of the expression "the gates of paradise." His expression became as great as the painting itself. Let that kind of feeling toward other people be ours. What kind of a life are we painting before others? What kind of details in the masterful strokes of Christ in our lives are we portraying? Let them be tempered by the strokes of the love of God, which tells us love is not jealous.

## Application

We have already alluded to 1 John 4:14: "We love, because He first loved us." This verse appears in the context of a Christian hating another Christian. That is why the following verse says, "If someone says, 'I love God,' and hates his brother, he is a liar; for the one who does not love his brother whom he has seen, cannot love God whom he has not see."

Interestingly, the Apostle John utilizes 1 John 4:19 as the solution to such a problem. Likewise, this verse can be the solution to anyone's problem of jealousy. "We love because He first loved us." The key obviously is that we must get to work on convincing ourselves that *God does love us*! The rest shall be automatic.

But this is not all. In John 17:23, we read, "That the world may know that thou didst send me, and didst love them, *even as thou didst love me*." Isn't that amazing? See how much God loves us, as much as He loved His only begotten Son! Should not such a realization overwhelmingly cause us to love also?

We close this chapter with the helpful words of Goethe: "Against the superiority of another, the only remedy is love. The psychologically healthy person rejoices in the excellence of others. Objectively interested in whatever he is giving his life to, he is glad when a musician, teacher, administrator appears who is better than himself. Thereby the world is enriched and if he can admire and so share in the excellency he is enriched himself." As another put it, "A supervisor character is a public banquet to which we are all invited."

# LIFE MESSAGE 4

## *Love Does Not Brag*

I knew a certain Christian years ago who seemed to have a vice of forgiving people and he really seemed to enjoy it. As a matter of fact, after you asked his forgiveness, he would say something like the following, "Oh, I certainly will forgive you," and then he would add, "I was just praying this morning, and God showed me all the different sufferings I must endure for His glory and the means by which I can grow to grace." That type of attitude alone was bad enough, but more than that, in the presence of other people he would refer to that forgiveness again. Numerous times the little incident that was supposedly forgiven by him was brought up in a sort of casual way. The meaning was plain. He seemed to take a double delight, on the one hand, in showing his great spirituality by forgiving people and on the other hand in exposing the restricted, hidden, secret things a person does wrong and in betraying the confidences. This person did not really know how to forgive, and he also was a braggart.

## I. The Ramifications of Bragging

Bragging takes all sorts of forms in life. It is not just saying "I did this great thing" or "I did that great thing." That is only one form of it. There are many other subtle ramifications, as we shall discover from 1 Corinthians 13:4, where Paul used a very interesting word to describe bragging. The fourth ingredient of love is a negative one. "Love does not brag." The word used for *brag* does not have one single meaning. John Calvin in his commentary on this passage says this word means "to display oneself; it means to boast; it means to brag; it means to talk about oneself repeatedly; it means to misbehave; it means to act unruly; it means to trouble people; it means to be inconsiderate." You will find a similar list of meanings in other commentaries and lexicons.

What does this mean? It means that bragging is something that has many ramifications.

Consider some of them. For example: self-deception. A little girl went to her priest in the confessional booth and said, "Oh, Father, I have to confess that I must be very, very proud."

He said, "Why?"

She replied, "Well, every morning I wake up and I look into the mirror and I see my face and I think to myself how beautiful I am."

And he said back to her, "Now just calm down, little girl. Don't worry, that's not so much pride as it is self-deception!"

Think this principle through and apply it. Perhaps we do the same thing once in a while too. The mirror is God's Word. Sometimes we look into it and we don't see what we should see. We go away, forgetting what good we think we saw, or what bad we saw.

Another ramification of bragging is vanity. One time Goethe and Beethoven were going for a little stroll through the park. They were talking about music. As they were walking together, people would come along and tip their hats, or give them a nice gesture and bow. This continued on throughout their walk. Finally, Goethe said, "This is too much for me to bear, all these people doing all this kind of homage." Beethoven just gave him a little word of rebuke by saying, "Perhaps a few of those are for me?"

Bragging is also self-seeking. A self-seeking individual is a braggart. The way people pursue status symbols is a definite form of bragging. They don't say, "Look at what great things I have done." But by the houses they live in, by the cars they drive, by the clothes they wear, by whatever they do to grab on to symbols that set forth their status in life, they are bragging.

Once an African Christian went to the village shoemaker and said he wanted a pair of shoes. He had them fitted exactly to his feet. He walked away very happily, and for weeks he wore those shoes. However, then he came back and said, "I want to return these."

The shoemaker asked him, "What's wrong with the shoes?"

He said, "Nothing, they fit perfectly."

"Well, then why don't you want them?"

"It's because they don't squeak"

The shoemaker couldn't understand the man's reasoning.

Obviously, it appeared to be that this Christian wanted to wear a pair of shoes that squeaked as he walked down the church aisle so that everybody would turn and look at him. It was a subtle way of bragging.

Another ramification of bragging is concept. Some people do not openly brag about themselves, but they show an attitude of coldness. You do not dare upset them in any way because if you do, all sorts of words will come forth from an injured, conceited attitude. Many of those words will be about how you hurt him. On the other hand, if the Christian gets to the point of realizing that he has no rights at all, you really cannot hurt him because he cannot stand up for rights he does not have.

Bragging is also a form of self-defensiveness. For example, a husband and wife both have learned to do things well. They never talk about their accomplishments, but if there is a slight hint of criticism in their conversation, something the one did not like in the other, before you know it, they are defending themselves from attack. In defending themselves, they really are telling each other how great they are. Is that also not another form of bragging?

What about being contentious? What about the person who always has to prove his point, or champion an issue? What really is the motive behind this? Is it perhaps a deflated ego, a person who wants to become inflated by winning an argument? Of course, often this person finds that when you win the argument, you so often lose the sale; when you win the argument, you lose the person involved. So what good does it do?

John Short brought out in his work on the passage that the most unpopular person in the world is a braggart. The person that people want to avoid the most is the one who talks about himself.

## II. The Reason behind Bragging

There are reasons why people brag.

### *A. The Apparent and Surface Reasons—Superiority*

At first glance, you would think that a person brags because he is superior to other people. This is true of many people who brag; they do accomplish big things and good things. Of course, they never learn that a person who has the right to brag does not need to, as Ben Franklin said. But, nevertheless, they go on.

*B. The Subtle and Real Reason—Inferiority*

But there is another, more subtle reason why people brag. It is for the opposite reason. Instead of having a superiority complex, they have an inferiority complex. Why is it that a person really needs to talk about how good he is? Why? Is it not because of his terrible feelings of inferiority, or inadequacy, and insecurity and fear? These people feel inadequate in the presence of other people who have superior talents.

1. Feeling of inadequacy before others.

They have a psychological need to talk to make up for their own deficiencies in contrast to what they see in the other person. They raise their own egos and do not feel so inferior after bragging.

2. Feeling of insecurity before God.

Some people also have great feelings of insecurity before God. A person who really does not know the love of God, and who really does not know how to trust in the Lord, needs to talk about himself and display himself, even in status symbols. By the way of contrast, think of Jesus Christ. He did not need more than one coat to wear; He did not have a place to lay His head; He did not need to have any of this world's possessions or riches. He walked by faith and not by sight, and yet He never felt insecure. But today there are so many Christians who have to get so many things for themselves just to feel a little bit of security.

3. Feeling of fear toward oneself.

Another aspect of inferiority in a person who has to brag is a feeling of fear toward himself. Listen to the person who has to brag; look at the person who trusts so much in status symbols, and mark it well that that person is afraid of himself. Afraid, for example, that what he is, underneath all of his talk and all of his status symbols, will be exposed if he stops talking and displaying himself. He is afraid, most of all, that he will see himself as he really is.

It has been well said, "The show-off is the one most shown-up in a showdown." There it is. The person with a great fear toward himself is always afraid that will happen.

Then there is Don Marquis' story about Wattie the Toad. He is the toad who felt that the world owed him everything. Finally, when the world provided a toadstool for him to be under, he said, "What did the universe do to deserve me?" Of course, that is perhaps rather extreme, but Wattie the Toad illustrates the attitudes of many of us. "Why did this church deserve me?" "What did this home do to deserve me?" On and on we go. Of course, the person who thinks that way, even to a certain degree, is nothing really more than a "toad."

## III. The Remedy of Bragging

We go on to the remedy for bragging. May I suggest three ways to solve the problem?

### *A. Reflect on the Past Experiences*

First of all, think about yourself. At least one of the above ramifications of bragging applies to you. As it has well been said, there is no vice that is more common with the average person, and yet more overlooked in his life, than the vice of bragging in one of its forms or another. So do not think of anyone else—think of yourself right now. Reflect on your past experience. Think clearly about how many experiences you can add to those I have already listed. See yourself as you really are.

*B. Remember the Scriptures*

Second, remember the scriptures. Look at Proverbs 25:27, for example. This is a very significant text with regard to the matter of bragging. "It is not good enough to eat much honey, nor is it glory to search out one's own glory." That is a paradox, is not it? Why do we do it? Why do we display ourselves in any form at all? Because we are seeking some glory; we are seeking some recognition to fulfill a great psychological need we have. But God says it is not glory to search out one's own glory.

Consider Proverbs 27:2: "Let another praise you and not your own mouth; a stranger and not your own lips." We are afraid that if we don't speak and tell how good we are, we'll be overlooked, and yet the Bible says even a stranger will recognize how good we are. Let them do it; don't do it for yourself.

In Matthew 23:12, Jesus says, "And whoever exalts himself shall be humbled or abased; and whoever humbles himself shall be exalted." That is a law of the universe. If in any way, shape, or form you brag, mark it well that you have already abased yourself; rather God will abase you because of it, and other people will too. There is no greater bore in all the world than a person who talks about himself. If you are like that, you will bore people to death, and that is why they will avoid you. But the reverse is true; if you humble yourself, you shall be exalted.

We read in 1 Peter 5:5–7, "The younger men will likewise be subject to your elders and all of you clothe yourselves with humility toward one another; for God is opposed to the proud, but God gives grace to the humble. Humble yourselves, therefore, under the mighty hand of God that He may exalt you at the proper time. Casting all your anxiety upon Him because He cares for you." How important this is! Are you afraid or are you worried about uncertainties in this life? Are you afraid you will be recognized for who you are? Cast all that on Him, and realize it is God's job to exalt you; it is not yours, nor does it belong to anyone else.

### *C. Realize the Essence of Love*

The last point is, after reflection on past experiences and remembering the scriptures, realize the essence of love. Turn to Philippians 2:1–5 and look carefully at the portrait of Jesus Christ found here. Notice what the apostle says in exclamatory terms: "If there is any encouragement in Christ, if there is any consolation of love…" Love is the only cure for a braggart. Love is the only cure for a person who has feelings of inferiority, insecurity, and fear. Just as there are many ramifications of bragging, there also are many ramifications of love to solve the problem of bragging. All the ramifications are found in verse 1. What is the answer? "Make my joy complete by being of the same mind, maintaining the same love, united in Spirit, intent on one purpose. Do nothing from selfish or empty conceit but with humility of mind, let each of you regard one another as more important than himself. Do not merely look out for your own personal interests but also for the interests of others. Have this attitude in yourselves which was also in Christ Jesus."

There it is. We violate the scriptures when we start talking about ourselves instead of others. We violate God's laws when we think of ourselves before the other person, when we think more of ourselves than we do of the other person. If we do this, we will wind up feeling all the more insecure, all the more inferior, and all the more afraid. Therefore, if you are a person who has feelings of inferiority, may I suggest the way to feel more superior? If that is what you really want, God's way is to think more highly of the other person and talk about him instead of yourself. Do you feel insecure? God will exalt you; you abase yourself and humble yourself. Do you feel afraid? There is great security, trust, and peace in the love that casts out all fear.

Love would correct bragging because it produces a desire for others to be happy. Love regards others with esteem; it teaches us to treat them with affectionate regard. No man who has affectionate regard for others is disposed to boast of his own qualities over them. Besides, love produces a state of mind just the opposite of a disposition to boast. It receives its endowments with gratitude, regards them as the gift of God, and is disposed to employ them not in vain boasting, but in purposes of utility, in doing good to all others on as wide a scale as possible. Christian love is humble. A truly great person never makes a display of his greatness. On the contrary, as John Short has phrased it, they "are so sure of themselves in their humble, gentle way that they do not need to attract attention to themselves. They indulge in no self-advertisement. If they are Christian, they are always willing and even anxious that their life and service should express not themselves but the spirit of the Master. Love's humility is its greatness. It is never boastful."

As Henry Drummond put it, "Love is our only salvation. Love which is superior to eloquence, to spiritual insight, to knowledge, to faith and even to charity and martyrdom; love which suffers long and is kind, is the only power in the world which can save a man from ridiculous swagger of boastfulness or from indulging himself in the bitter sneers of envy, for it neither grudges others of their gifts nor is it eager to show off its own. Love has not only the positive virtue of being patient and kind, but it also saves a man from making a fool of himself by pompous conduct.

"And then, having learned all that, you have to learn this further thing: humility—to put a seal upon your lips and forget what you have done. After you have fruitfully used your gifts, after you have accomplished something great, after you have been patient and kind, after your love has stolen forth into the world and done its beautiful work, go back again into the shade and say nothing about it. Love hides even from itself. Love waives even self-satisfaction. Love does not display itself.

"Love destroys boastfulness. When love really goes to work in a Christian, it so takes possession that it transforms pride into humility, insecurity into security, selfishness into selflessness. And this is not so amazing because what has happened is that the center of spiritual gravity has been changed from self to Christ. Love, true love, will limit our esteem for ourselves and prevent the tumors of self-display?"

**Application**

A young man was in the theater of Athens, during the days of the great Greek philosophers, standing around saying, "I have become wise because I have talked to so many wise men!"

But Epictetus stood up, and with his great years of wisdom and age, said, "Young man, not necessarily so, for I have talked to many rich men, but I'm not rich?"

Reading these words alone will not stop you from bragging. As the old saying goes, "Talk is cheap. Listening is better, but practicing is best of all!"

# LIFE MESSAGE 5

## *Love Is Not Arrogant*

"Love is patient, love is kind, and is not jealous; love does not brag and is not arrogant" (1 Cor. 13:4). In the King James Version, the words *puffed up* are used for arrogant. Those words remind me of the first fish my friend caught when his dad took him deep-sea fishing. As a boy of eight, it was a big thrill for him, even though he only caught a blowfish. Do you know what a blowfish is? When you pull it out of the water and scratch its belly, it puffs up like a balloon. This is the mental image I get when I read, "Love is not arrogant." Of course, what we are really talking about here is pride. In this chapter, we want to consider from God's Word how pride causes us to be arrogant, how it causes us to be puffed up just like a blowfish. Our pride puffs us up because we seek to protect ourselves too. Our study on love at this point forces us to think about the whole matter of pride.

When you think of a person who is arrogant, you probably think of a very outgoing person, a braggadocio, one who is very forceful and overbearing, and this is true in many cases. However, other kinds of people can be just as proud. There is not one of us who does not have some degree of pride in our lives. Since God's Word says love is not arrogant, we cannot allow pride to be in our lives if we want God's love to fill us.

It is necessary to look at arrogance from four viewpoints: 1) the root of arrogance, 2) the ramifications of arrogance, 3) the results of arrogance, and 4) the removal of arrogance.

## I. The Root of Arrogance

Pride works within us to shut us off from God. It shuts us off from the kind of love that God seeks to pour into us. Pride really strives within each one of us, blinding us to the fact that we really are sinners. Many people, of course, recognize they are sinners. That is why they accept Jesus Christ. And they know that they still commit sinful acts. But the question is whether we really consider ourselves to be sinners. "Yes, I commit sins," we say, but are we sinners? Or does our pride blind us to that fact that we really are sinners?

### *A. Inner Striving of Pride*

Many times we center our attention on the things in our lives that are wrong, that are an affront to God, the things that are sinful. But we need to realize the root of sinful acts, that we are in a state of being sinful people. This is what Jesus Christ came to redeem us from, from the state of being sinful people. We are still sinners, even though saved by grace. All of us are by nature sinners. It is pride in us that strives to cause us to overlook this fact. Consequently, to some degree, we are all proud and arrogant because we do not really recognize the fact that in and of ourselves we are sinners. This is part of our nature; this is part of our being. Pride strives to blind us to this fact.

*B. Deception of Pride*

Pride also deceives us and causes us to be arrogant. Often when we do recognize sin in our lives, the guilt comes. But the guilt comes when we experience the consequences of our sin, rather than the sin itself. One of the things that holds back God's blessing in our lives is the fact that we really do not fear God. If we really did fear God, we would call sin "sin" when we see it in our lives. We would call it sin and not wait until the consequences set in. We would refrain from because it t is an affront to God. Pride causes us to feel guilty about the consequences of sin, rather than the in itself. This is because pride stirs up our concern about our appearance before other people. Pride puts up a front and keeps other people from seeing us as we really are.

*C. Inner Distortions of Pride*

In many ways, pride distorts our image of God. Because God is the creator of the universe, He also wants to be King in our lives. There's a logical deduction. But pride many times causes us not to allow God to be God in our lives. Pride tricks us into thinking that God is really King in our lives, when in reality we are on the throne and we are calling the shots. We are having our own way. That is arrogance.

In Galatians 5:19–21, we see some of the visible symptoms of pride: "Now the deeds of the flesh are evident, which are immorality, impurity, sensuality, idolatry, sorcery, enmities, strife, jealousy, outbursts of anger, disputes, dissension, factions, envyings, drunkenness, carousings and things like these of which I forewarn you just as I have forewarned you that those who practice such things shall not inherit the kingdom of God." That is a portrait of our nature. It is a description of every one of us, whether we are practicing these things overtly or not. These things are characteristic of every man. That is why God says there is none that is righteous; we have all gone astray; no one seeks God because by nature, we are sinful (Rom. 3:11–12). We do not need to be reformed; we need to be liberated from ourselves so that Jesus Christ can flow through us.

### *D. Final Consequences of Pride*

Pride produces these visible symptoms because we allow self to have its own way. That's arrogance. The final consequence of pride is that it causes us to be hardened to sin. When we allow ourselves to be on the throne of our lives, when we satisfy ourselves, we begin to grow hardened even to the sin that the Spirit of God convicts us of. When He reproves us, we turn our backs. As we continue to turn our backs, we become hardened to sin. Our arrogance before God hardens us eventually to the point where we will call right wrong, and wrong right. That is what pride does. Such is an arrogant person.

## II. The Ramifications of Arrogance

Now let us consider some of the ramifications of arrogance so that we can identify it in our lives.

### *A. Pride*

At the top of the list is pride itself. Pride is the essence of arrogance. Pride is excessive self-esteem, putting myself above all else, even above God Himself.

*B. Haughtiness*

Another ramification of pride is a haughty spirit. What does it mean to have a haughty spirit? It means to be conscious of your own superior birth or your own superior power. It means looking down on other people because they are not of the same social class as you, or they do not have the same means as you. Because you perceive yourself as powerful and influential, you have a haughty attitude toward those of a lower status.

*C. Lordliness*

An arrogant person is a lordly person, one who pompously displays his power. All of us have others who look up to us. But how do we display this relationship? Are we lordly with our power? Are we like possessive little children? You take your children to visit Johnny, and suddenly little Johnny becomes very possessive with his toys. You do not have to teach him that. He lords it over his playmates; he lets them know what they can have and what they cannot have. This is part of our sinful nature. This is the way we are without God and without Christ.

*D. Insolence*

Arrogance makes us insolent. Often we become insolent to the point of actually despising other people. There are people we just do not like to be around. There are people with whom we are not comfortable. Maybe you consider yourself above them! This is insolence.

*E. Forcefulness*

An arrogant person is overbearing, he forces himself on other people, and he is tyrannical in his manner.

*F. Supercilious*

Another ramification of arrogance is the supercilious expression as seen in the uplifted eyebrow and the permeating attitude of a cool, condescending spirit.

*G. Scorn*

Arrogance makes us disdainful of others. It leads to scorning other people because of the way they are, because of the way they look, because of the way they act. This attitude often comes out when we talk with our husbands and wives and our friends about other people.

*H. Conceit*

Conceit is another ramification of arrogance. This is an excessive appreciation of our own virtues, our own abilities. It centers in ourselves and elevates ourselves.

*I. Self-Righteousness*

Self-righteousness is another ramification of arrogance. If we look at this list of nine ramifications of arrogance, we are sure to find something that applies to some degree. It is our nature to be arrogant; it is our nature to be proud. This is an indication of the fact that we are sinners.

## III. The Results of Arrogance

What are the results of arrogance in our lives? How does it affect our relationship with God?

### *A. In Our Relationship with God*

Allow the scripture to speak for itself:

"In pride the wicked hotly pursues the afflicted. Let them be caught in the plots which they have devised. For the wicked boasts of his heart's desire, and the greedy man curses and spurns the Lord" (Ps. 10:2–3).

"May the Lord cut off all flattering lips, great the tongue that speaks great things" (Ps. 12:3).

"No one who has a haughty look and an arrogant heart will I endure" (Ps. 101:5).

"For though the Lord is exalted, yet He regards the lowly, but the haughty He knows from afar" (Ps. 138:6).

"Everyone who is proud in heart is an abomination to the Lord. Assuredly, he will not be unpunished" (Prov. 16:18–19).

"A rich man's wealth is his strong city, and like a high wall in his own imagination. Before destruction, the heart of man is haughty, but humility goes before honor" (Prov. 18:11–12).

The word of the Lord speaks very clearly that God does not honor a haughty spirit; God does not honor pride. Pride cuts us off from God. Pride shuts us off from the free flow of God's Spirit. Love is not arrogant. Love opens us up to God and allows God to be God in our lives.

### *B. In Our Relationships with Others*

Another result of arrogance is the fact that it cuts us off from other people. It causes us to think poorly of them. We begin to devalue them as people. It causes us to think poorly of them. We begin to devalue them as people. We begin to devalue their gifts because their gifts may be a threat to us, to our being esteemed by others.

Pride also causes us to devalue other people's needs. God has placed us on this earth to be ministers to one another, but pride keeps us from being sensitive to other people's needs. It cuts off our awareness of their needs. God wants to use us to meet other people's needs, but if we are self-centered, we can't be used. We become more interested in satisfying our own desires because of arrogance.

Pride causes us not to be transparent with people, not to be open with them, because we are afraid they will see us as we really are. But love is not that way. Love is allowing yourself to be seen as you really are, by God's grace. On the other hand, arrogance shuts us off from what God is seeking to do in other people's lives. Every acquaintance we have is a "divine encounter." This is because God is seeking to work in the lives of others through us. When I come together with another person, I should ask myself, what is God doing in this person's life, and what can I do to help God accomplish this? But if there is arrogance in our lives, we cannot minister to other people because we are more interested in our own needs being met.

### *C. In Our Relationship to Ourselves*

Arrogance also keeps us in bondage to ourselves. That is the opposite of humility. Real humility is being full of God, but if we are arrogant, we are full of ourselves. We are in bondage to ourselves when we do not allow God to be God in our lives.

Being arrogant means being unable to give up our rights to God because we must protect them. We must do all we can to see that our needs wants and desires are met. This is why being arrogant keeps us from experiencing the joy of surrendering our rights to God. If we are arrogant, we do not allow God to take over our lives and to protect us. This is His responsibility, once we give our rights back to Him. So the root of arrogance is pride; the ramifications involve all of us; the results of arrogance cut us off from God; they cut us off from other men; and we are in bondage to ourselves.

## IV. The Removal of Arrogance

But how do we get rid of arrogance?

### *A. Abasement before God*

Before we can experience freedom from ourselves, before we can experience freedom from arrogance, we must abase ourselves before God and recognize that indeed we are sinners. Recognize that without Him, we are nothing! We are truly nothing. Our lives are empty without Him, and we must abase ourselves before Him.

### *B. Attitude of Christ*

One of the ways we can remove arrogance is to seek the kind of humility that Jesus Christ had when He came to John the Baptist. John said, "Behold, the Lamb of God who takes away the sin of the world." The kind of disposition that God is looking for in each one of us *is* the disposition of a lamb, willing to be shorn. A lamb does not complain when he loses his wool. He is willing to give up His rights. We need to get a vision of Jesus the Lamb if we are going to rid ourselves of arrogance. We need to have the kind of spirit He had. When He was baptized, a dove came down and rested upon Him, a picture of gentleness and peace. This is the disposition God expects in each one of us. If we are going to remove arrogance, He wants us to have the disposition of a lamb, of a dove, so we can be gentle and peaceable.

*C. Rule of Peace*

In Colossians 3:15 Paul says, "And let the peace of Christ rule in your hearts to which indeed you were called in one body, and be thankful." The Spirit of God came upon Jesus as a symbol of peace. Because we are baptized by the Spirit into the body of Jesus Christ, the peace of God ought to be in us. Because we have peace with God, therefore, we ought to know the peace of God. When the peace of God stops flowing, it's an indication that arrogance has come in somewhere. God expects His peace to rule in our lives. When it is not there, something is wrong; the lamb-like disposition, or Jesus, is not in us. If we yield to His peace, we shall find that love *is* not arrogant. But if there is arrogance, we cannot experience His peace. Where do we start to experience the removal of arrogance from our lives?

*D. Begin in Your Home*

The best place to start is in our homes. This is where it is most difficult to give up our rights. This is where it is most difficult not to display pride. This is where we react most often to selfishness and pride in other people. But we can start by recognizing qualities that God wants in our lives—those lamb-like, dove-like qualities. Perhaps our rights will be violated when we seek to be humble, when we seek to abase ourselves before God, when we seek to yield to others in our homes. Perhaps God will put us to the test to see how sincere we are about giving up our nights and removing pride and arrogance.

Perhaps He will not change others in your family first. You may have to take the first step. We cannot wait for perfect situations to develop. We must look at each situation as an opportunity to develop the kind of qualities that God wants in our lives. This means being a true servant of others in our families. Rather than react to them, respond to them and allow the love of God to flow through you.

*E. Willingness to Serve*

Another way to remove arrogance is to adopt the attitude of a bondslave. Jesus took that attitude toward His disciples. Therefore, we also ought to look for ways to serve others. There was no arrogance when Jesus Christ washed the feet of the disciples. Did he not deserve esteem? Yes. Did He not deserve to have His abilities recognized? Yes. Did He not deserve to have His right honored? Yes. But Jesus Christ was a servant. He was a bondslave to the will of God in His life. He set an example for us to be bondslaves as well. This means allowing God to be God in our lives, not ourselves, not our pride, not our arrogance. Being a bondservant means allowing ourselves to be taken advantage of by others in the family. If we are practicing "love is not arrogant," we will get some responsibilities thrown on us that normally arc not ours. We can expect not to receive a thank you when we do things out of love for people because love is not arrogant, love is not proud, and love does not seek its own.

We are bondslaves, and we have no rights as bondslaves because we have given up our rights to Jesus Christ. This will mean being stretched to the limit. It will mean allowing our rights to be violated while we maintain a dove-like, lamb-like quality. It will mean not lashing back at someone, not reacting.

We have been saved to be servants. And when we are anything else but servants, we are not fulfilling God's will for our lives, but we are thwarting the love of God in our lives. We are not allowing our lives to be opened to the free flow of God's Spirit. We are not allowing our lives to be open to the flow of God's love through us.

*F. Appropriate "the Blood"*

We noted above that we must abase ourselves before God and recognize that we are sinners. Then we accept God's love in Christ by taking to ourselves the blood of Jesus Christ, which cleanses us from all sin, even the sin of arrogance. The blood of Jesus Christ, a fountain that still flows, can cleanse us from all the ramifications of arrogance. Therefore, we must allow ourselves to be set free by appropriating the blood of Jesus Christ. Jesus Christ not only saved us for heaven after this life, He also saved us from the present power of sin. After we recognize our sin and call it sin, we can be purified. God purifies us with the blood of His Son. His blood cleanses us day by day, hour by hour, moment by moment, whenever we sin. This is the way to rid ourselves of arrogance.

**Application**

Then we can appropriate the free gift of God's love in Jesus Christ. First Corinthians 12 lists some of the gifts that God offers to His body, the church. But 1 Corinthians 13 talks about His greatest gift: the gift of love. These attributes of love can be true in our lives. But we need to appropriate that gift. When Jesus becomes Lord of our lives, then His nature becomes part of our nature, and we begin to manifest the fruit of God's Spirit in our lives. Our lives are characterized by humility, not by arrogance. God offers each one of us that free gift of love in Jesus Christ.

Allow the conviction of God's spirit to come upon you. Appropriate the blood in Jesus Christ to rid yourself of arrogance and pride so you can be the kind of person described in 1 Corinthians 13: "Love is not arrogant."

Love is humble, love is being a bondslave, love is being willing to serve.

# LIFE MESSAGE 6

## *Love Does Not Act Unbecomingly*

There he is, standing in the snow. The snowflake destroyed his world power. He was a great man, and he still remains great in the eyes the world. But this great man and his armies were defeated by a snowflake. Was he really the man he thought he was? No. That's why he was an arrogant man. That's why he stands in that famous posture. Napoleon stands with all his arrogance and pride.

Napoleon? The great general, the great leader, the world emperor an arrogant man? Yes, he was a great man in many ways, but also, among other things, he was arrogant. Because he was arrogant, he also was very discourteous. Many times he acted very unbecomingly, he knew very little about how to live in style. He could force people out of duty but not inspire them inwardly. That is why he treated his soldiers the way he did.

In the previous chapter, we dealt with arrogance. This is not another chapter on that subject. But arrogance is intimately related to things like courtesy, acting becomingly, having style in the way we come across to people.

Our understanding of the apostle's description of love is hindered by the break between verses 4 and 5 of 1 Corinthians 13. The last word of verse 4 is *arrogant*, and verse 5 goes on "does not act unbecomingly." One would think that because of the verse break that there is no logical connection between being arrogant and acting unbecomingly. But we cannot make that conclusion; the opposite is true. Arrogance and acting unbecomingly are very intimately related. A person who is arrogant, a person who has a puffed up estimation of himself, cannot be sensitive to the feelings, interests, and rights of other people; arrogant people think so highly of themselves that they cannot condescend to little old people like you or me. It is very difficult for an arrogant person to act in a becoming way. Arrogance is the cause of discourtesy, the cause of bad manners, and the cause of a lack of style.

We use words like *courtesy*, *good manners*, *kindness*, and *style* because they are all related to the idea of acting unbecomingly. I want to use the word *style* as an umbrella word for all these concepts. The dictionary says *style* means "a distinctive, particular mode of behavior or deportment." When we say "That person has style!" what we mean is "He has a good way of coming across that really turns us on."

But how does a person get that? This way of coming across in a becoming way is something that we ought to have as Christians. Paul says, "Yes, love does not act unbecomingly." I want you to note three dimensions in life concerning style. There are three kinds of Christian responses to this word. First of all, there are some Christians who deny style. They live as though it has nothing to do with their Christian lives. Second, there are some who doubt style. And third, there are some who develop style. This third category should be the goal for all of us.

## I. Denying Style

We must begin by asking ourselves which dimension we are in. Do we deny style, not by our thoughts, but by the way we talk, by the way we come across, by the way we are observed by other people? Do you go through life denying style? Are you one who goes through life doubting style? Or do you want to go through life developing it?

### *A. The Relationship of Arrogance and Rudeness*

First, let's take the one who goes through life denying style. This person evidences a relationship between arrogance and rudeness. There is arrogance in his life. He has never overcome the basic problem of puffed-up pride, a high opinion of himself. Because of this, he cannot possibly be sensitive about people's feelings, their interests, their rights, and his obligations to them. He is the center of his own world, which has the consequential effect of turning people off. Do you have that problem?

In 1 Corinthians 13:11, Paul says, "When I was a child, I used to speak as a child, think as a child, reason as a child, but when I became a man, I did away with childish things."

### *B. The Relevance of Childishness and Rudeness*

A second reason why people go through life denying style is because they are childish. A child of four, rushing into a room, screaming at the top of his lungs, demanding instant attention, cannot understand that he is wrong for doing such things. He cannot possibly be aware that his actions unnerve adults and cause instant tension. A child sees himself as the center of his universe; everything in life revolves around him and his demands. A little child cannot understand that other people are as important, if not more important, as him.

Paul said, "When I became a man I put away childish things." Yet many Christians have not put away childish things; they wonder why they upset people.

*C. The Realization of True Greatness and Rudeness*

A third reason why Christians go through life out of style is because they do not understand what true greatness is. What is it? Stand back from 1 Corinthians 13 and try to get an overall view of the chapter. What do you see? You see a portrait of living Christ. When Paul, inspired by the Holy Spirit, wrote those qualities of life, he must have thought of the one whom he adored above all: the Lord Jesus Christ.

Jesus represents true greatness. It was not until my sixth year of graduate school that I realized that 1 Corinthians 13 wasn't a beautiful exposition on love but rather a portrait of Christ Himself. Why? Because I was tuned out as to what true greatness was. My eyes of perception could not grasp what was really out there.

As Henry Drummond put it, "Love is so great that it never calls attention to itself; so much so, that after it has done its great task, whatever its task is, it not only hides from the praise of others and response of others, and the recognition of others, but it even hides from itself as it goes back into the shade into total humility and self-abasement."

One reason we go through life denying style, turning people off instead of turning them on, is because we do not understand true greatness.

What a contrast. Napoleon stands in history with all his great posture of arrogance. But where is Jesus? We have to be told that His portrait is in 1 Corinthians 13. Why? He doesn't draw attention to Himself. That is true greatness. When we get to that point in our Christian lives, that whatever we think, say, and do, we do for the glory of God instead of other people, then we will have learned true greatness and we shall be on the road toward living in God's style.

## II. Doubting Style

But perhaps you are the kind of Christian who goes through life doubting style. Why should a Christian go through life doubting style? There are two basic reasons: 1) because of a great concern for truth, and 2) because of an undue concern about testing, temptation, and trials.

### *A. Because of a Concern for the Truth*

There are some Christians who are so concerned about accuracy of truth that they lose all Christian grace. For instance, a lady just arrived home from church. She walked into her house very hurt. Why? Because she was troubled by two seminary graduates whom she loved very much. After the service, she had said something that was perhaps a bit untheological. In response, the two seminary men smiled and looked at each other knowingly. They knew her terminology wasn't quite right. They acted as though they were entertained, or perhaps even offended by it. And so the woman went home very hurt. Later, she wrote of these two young men, "They lacked style." They were so concerned for the truth and its accuracy that they failed their duty of love to this woman.

A second reason why some Christians are so concerned for the truth is that they want to be accepted by the in-crowd. An unfortunate thing that often happens to a new Christian is that he loses the freshness of his prayer expressions when he realizes his prayer method is not identical to that used by the in-crowd. So he gradually adapts, and before long, he sounds like the rest of the Christians, the in-crowd. If we are concerned about conforming our ways to that of the in-crowd, we will lose our unique style, a style that God wants to use to bless the hearts of people.

Some people are overly concerned for the truth because they are afraid of becoming liberal. In my own education for the ministry, I have often heard professors say that liberals emphasize love and conservatives emphasize truth. I began to think that if I would actually become more loving, I would be mistaken for a liberal! So I avoided it like a disease. That is a fact.

A marvelous cure for all this can be found in John 1:14. This is another portrait of Christ penned by John. "And the Word became flesh and dwelt among us, and we beheld His glory, glory as of the only begotten from the Father, full of grace and truth." The word *grace*, by the way, is the word that can also be translated to "charm." "Charm" is what we mean by the use of the word *style*. Christ was full of style and truth, full of charm and truth. He attracted people so they craved what He had. In the Greek, the word is in the emphatic position: "full of grace (charm, style) and truth." Christ did not emphasize love, grace, or style at the expense of truth, but neither did He emphasize truth at the expense of losing love, charm, and style. He was a balanced man; He was full of both. He was full of style of truth. What a tremendous corrective for us. We become so overly concerned about truth that we neglect to be loving.

### *B. Because of a Concern for Testing*

When it comes to testings, we sometimes go through life doubting the importance and priority of style. Sometimes we get so overly preoccupied with the test, or trial, or temptation that we miss the importance of love. We pass the test to the letter of the law but lack love. "I can't lie." But in not lying, we can be very ungracious. Or "I can't steal. I can't do a thing like that." In saying that very thing, we can be so arrogant that we forsake love. Even in our obedience to witnessing correctly, we can be very unloving.

In stressing perfection, we often ignore style. Or if we have a melancholy temperament, we excuse ourselves for a lack of love. Or if we have a bad temper.

In James 1:2, we find a corrective concerning temptations and tests. "Consider it all joy, my brethren." Some Christians, when they face a temptation, trial, or test, pray for patience. God sends them that test to give them patience. But God also says, "Consider it all joy." This is the style of love. "Brethren, when you encounter various trials knowing that the testing of your faith produces endurance." Endurance is nothing more than love having style to the end. Whatever the test is, it is for the purpose of increasing your love, not just to have you put up with it, but to do so with grace and style. "Let endurance have its perfect result that you may be perfect and complete, lacking in nothing," especially in style.

So whatever the test, you can meet it in style, being courteous and mannerly. Let me give you a specific about style. I quote Henry Drummond, who said, "Courtesy or good manners is nothing more than love in tiny things." Try that and see the style of the Spirit of God with all His fruit flow through your life in abundance. Acting becomingly is loving people in small things.

## III. Developing Style

There is a third group: those who are developing style. To see something of what we mean by this, look at the beloved poet, Robert Burns. He was called the Plowman Poet because he was loved so much by ordinary people. It was said that he could walk into a cottage of a widow, or the mansion of a king, and be at home and in style in both realms. Why? Because he loved the mouse whose nest was plowed up in the field. He loved the daisy on the hillside. He loved every little thing and every big thing that God created. Robert Burns was called the greatest gentleman in Europe. He knew what it meant to cultivate or develop style. Thank God for some Christians who actually have matured so much that they have developed style. Of course, the most mature Christian will tell you he has never arrived in his manners, courtesy, kindness, love, and style so that he can stop developing. He is always involved in cultivating his love and style. Regardless of what level you are on today, if you want to continue to develop your love beyond where you are now, you should consider the four steps below.

### *A. Process of Growth*

Step number 1: realize the process of growth. Second Peter 3:18 commands us, "But grow in the grace and knowledge of our Lord and Savior Jesus Christ." Believers are expected to grow spiritually just like children physically. This means good manners, courtesy, and kindness, among other things. Having style involves growth.

Second Peter 1:5–7 lists the building blocks of growth, or the baby steps of faith to grow up in Jesus Christ. If you want to grow step by step, and learn how to walk better as a Christian, may I suggest these little steps mentioned here:

"Now for this very reason also, applying all diligence, in your faith, supply moral excellence, and in your moral excellence, knowledge and in your knowledge, self-control, and in your self-control, perseverance; and in your perseverance, godliness; and in your godliness, brotherly kindness; and in your brotherly kindness, Christian love." If you follow these steps, you will have a developing style. This is growth.

*B. Practicality of Decisions*

Step number 2: the practicality of decisions. Proverbs 3:5–6 says, "Trust in the Lord with all your heart and lean not to your own understanding," in all your ways, in all your decisions. Decisions, decisions, decisions. In one day, there are a thousand decisions to make. Whether to go be kind or cruel. Whether to work hard or take it easy. Whether to drive fast or slow. In all your decisions, acknowledge Him. Realize the practicality of your decisions; realize your love and your style will increase as you learn to decide between style and self.

*C. Power of Willingness*

Step number 3: You may say, "Look, I am the way I am. This is how I was made, and if you don't like it, leave it!" Have you ever heard anybody talk like that? I have. Anyone who talks like that is arrogant, especially in God's eyes. There was a time when I thought that way. A person who speaks like that knows nothing of Christ.

On the other hand, 2 Corinthians 8:12 says, "For if the readiness is present, it is acceptable according to what a man has, not according to what he does not have." If you tell me, "I just don't have those niceties. I can't be kind like that. I can't be loving in little tiny things. It's not me," then I say to you, as long as you are willing to change, God does not expect you to be something that you are not. The important thing is not what you do not have; it is what you are. In other words, just begin where you are and be willing for God to change you. You cannot make yourself over. But if you are a Christian, the person of the living Christ is in your being and He wants to burst into your life and make you a new creation.

Paul writes in 2 Corinthians 5:17, "Therefore if any man is in Christ, he is a new creature, the old things passed away, behold, new things have come." When a person is born again, he is not only saved from hell, he is also saved from himself. If you feel you can't be kind, courteous, gentlemanly, and mannerly, then claim that as an area in which Christ will save you. God is concerned with our being saved from the ugly sins in our lives that upset our wives, our husbands, our friends, and our children. He is also concerned if unbelievers are not impressed by our Christian profession, if they are not attracted by style.

After counseling four hours with a new couple, I learned what really attracted them to Jesus. It was not being saved from hell. They knew that was involved, but there was more to it than that. When they heard that Jesus saves us from the power of our sins, as well as from the penalty, that registered with them. When they realized that Christ could save them from their pride, from their stubborn wills, and from whatever sins in their lives from which they could not save themselves, they wanted to receive Him. They said, "We will pay the price to get that." And yet some Christians are still touchy about some things in their lives. Why?

Because they have never let Christ come into that area to save them from that sin.

How about you? Will you let Christ save you? Are you willing to say, "All right. I am miserable this way, but I am willing to let Christ save me from it, because I cannot do it myself."

*D. Practice of Obedience*

Step number 4: the practice of obedience. In John 14:15, we read, "If you love me, keep my commandments." After we experience salvation from sin, death, and hell, we can know the joy of being saved from our sins day by day. This victory comes by practicing obedience. Jesus Christ said, "My sheep hear my voice, and I know them, and they follow me." Do you hear His voice? Do you obey His commands? This is the way to develop a genuinely Christian lifestyle.

**Application**

There is a very simple conclusion to all of this. Those who lack good manners, etiquette, courtesy, style, and love in the tiny things need to be "saved" in those areas. George Washington must have known this truth. One day when he was walking down the path with Lafayette, he was greeted by a black slave who said, "Good morning, General." General Washington actually took off his hat, did a bow, and said, "Good morning to you." Noticing the quizzical smile on Lafayette, he turned to him and said, "My colleague, could I really let a black slave outdo me in good manners?" That is a mark of greatness. That is style; that is love. So great was Washington that he would not think of offending a slave. Christ was like that. Are you like that? Love does not act unbecomingly, for love has style.

# LIFE MESSAGE 7

## *Love Does Not Seek Its Own*

There he is, walking cockily into a multitude of people gathered around the Lord Jesus. He brushes people as he walks past them, trips over a few feet, hurries past some others in need of beings healed, and ignores the compassion he owes them. He stomps right into the presence of the disciples themselves, pushes them aside, and walks right over the Lord and Master Himself. With the arrogance of wealth and youth, what does he care about the rights of others? He demands of Jesus. "Sir, what must I do to inherit eternal life?"

To this rich young ruler, our Lord answered, "Keep all the commandments. You know them. Keep them."

And the rich young ruler said back to him, "But I have kept all these commandments since the days of my youth."

Then Christ said, "Oh, you have in so many words, then why do you ask Me, 'What must I do to inherit eternal life'?"

"Because I want to know from You what You think I should do to inherit eternal life."

Jesus made it clear. "All right, I'll tell you in so many words. Go, sell all your riches, give them to the poor, and then follow after Me."

The rich young ruler thought for a moment, bowed his head, and walked away with great shame because he knew that where his treasure was, his heart was also. His treasure happened to be his riches, not his faith in God.

We see a man insisting on his own way, but we also see the love of our Lord. Perhaps there were tears in His eyes because the scripture says, "He pitied him because of how greatly He loved him."

What a tragedy for the Lord Jesus Christ to love anyone, rich young ruler or not, only to have that person go his own way. Insisting on one's own way is not just peculiar to a rich man; rather it is a universal problem of human nature. All of us to one degree or another have a problem with insisting on our own way. We hold very closely to ourselves, not necessarily our riches, but our rights—what we think we deserve. We, to some degree, actually feel that the world owes us a living, that our wives owe us something, our children owe us something, our husbands owe us something, our parents owe us something, or the community does, or our friends. We all basically have that inner problem of wanting our own way. We look out for ourselves, even at the expense of others.

There are two basic kinds of selfish people: There are those who are overt in their selfishness, very crude, known by their rudeness, lack of manners and arrogance. When we meet them, we're glad we're not like them. The second type of selfish person is the one who is very subtle about his selfish desires. He knows that publicizing his selfish aims will turn people off, therefore he will be more quiet about it. He devises ways of secret maneuvering, manipulating people and things until he gets what he wants. On the surface, this person could appear to be the sweetest, kindest, and most loving person, but underneath, what is the real motive? Is this person not also selfish?

## I. Sincere Conflict between Selfishness and Self-Interest

The problem of selfishness is further compounded by another question: Is it always wrong to think of my needs? Don't I have any right to think of what I need in life, or to think about what I myself must be in order to help other people? We are caught on the horns of the dilemma. On the one side, is the problem of selfishness, and on the other, the problem of self-interest. These two sides constantly conflict with one another. *Selfishness* is defined as wanting your own way at the expense of other people or God. *Self-interest* is defined as wanting your own way for the benefit of God and other people. This may be illustrated, for example, by a lifeguard. He has to learn how to swim before he can save another from drowning. He must also learn life-saving skills so he will know what to do when a person is drowning. To save his own life, he needs to learn defensive procedures, in case the drowning person tries to grab him and pull him under. Is the lifeguard wrong for thinking of himself?

The Bible says in 1 Corinthians 13:5, "Love does not seek its own."

What about the housewife? Is it wrong for her to want proper sleep, proper food, and proper love from her husband? Is it wrong for her to expect tender care from him so that she in turn can be a good wife and mother? Is it wrong for the breadwinner of the family to expect his wife to treat him right and his children to make him happy? Is it wrong for him to want his food, clothing, and shelter all cared for when he comes home from work?

All these questions, you see, crop up in this conflict between selfishness and self-interest. How do we resolve them? Have we really sat down with the Word of God and looked for the answer from God to this problem of selfishness? I have found this to be a very difficult chapter. I have the problem of being basically selfish myself. I have been selfish in the ministry many times, and right in my own home. I need to learn from the Holy Spirit how to be less selfish. I'm writing, not because I have overcome all selfishness, but because this truth has to be presented.

## II. Solution to the Problem

The answer is found in four scriptures. Those simple words "Love does not seek its own way" must be expanded by other scripture texts. The greatest commentary on them is to be found in the Bible itself.

There are people in my congregation who have come to Christ through the truth of these scriptures about denying self, letting one's self die, and taking up one's cross and following Him. There are four accounts in the gospels where the same basic truth is taught, that if any man would like to follow Christ, he must first of all deny himself, pick up his cross, and follow Him. That same truth appears four times in the gospels in different contexts, and in answer to different questions. Taken together, they will help us solve the problem of selfishness.

### *A. Mark 8:31–38*

First, Mark 8:31–38. "And He began to teach them that the Son of man must suffer many things and be rejected by the elders and the chief priests and the scribes, and be killed, and after three days rise again. And He was stating the matter plainly. And Peter took Him aside and began to rebuke Him. But turning around and seeing His disciples, He rebuked Peter and said, 'Get behind Me, Satan; for you are not setting your mind on God's interests, but man's.' And He summoned the multitude with His disciples, and said to them, 'If anyone wishes to come after Me, let him deny himself, and take up his cross, and follow Me. For whoever wishes to save his life shall lose it; and whoever loses his life for My sake and the gospel's shall save it. For what does it profit a man to gain the whole world, and forfeit his soul? For what shall a man give in exchange for his soul? For whoever is ashamed of Me and My words in this adulterous and sinful generation, the Son of Man will also be ashamed of him when He comes in the glory of His Father with the holy angels.'"

Notice especially that the answer "deny yourself, take up your cross, and follow Me" was given to Peter in response to his rebuke of Jesus. In the face of Peter's thinking of man's interests, and not God's, Christ gave this statement, that a man should deny himself, take up his cross, and follow Him. Jesus added, "And whoever wants to save his life (his own way) shall (in essence) lose it, and whoever seeks to lose his life for Christ's sake shall find it."

*B. Luke 9:18–26*

Second, Luke 9:18–26. The words are essentially the same, but the situation is different. "And it came about that while He was praying alone, the disciples were with Him, and He questioned them saying, 'Who do the multitudes say that I am?'" The occasion here was one of prayer, and Jesus used a question to teach the disciples something concerning His identity. "And they answered and said, 'John the Baptist; but others say, Elijah; and others, that one of the prophets of old has risen again.' And He said to them, 'But who do you say that I am?' And Peter answered and said, 'The Christ of God.' But He warned them, and instructed them not to tell this to anyone, saying, 'The Son of Man must suffer many things, and be rejected by the elders and chief priests and scribes, and be killed, and be raised up on the third day.'"

Jesus prophesied His suffering, but He was praying before He told them these things. In Luke's account, Peter passed the test with the proper answer about who Christ was, but yet on the other hand, he flunked it because he rebuked the Lord. The rebuke is not recorded in Luke's account. Jesus continued, "If anyone wishes to come after Me, let him deny himself, and take up his cross daily and follow Me."

Jesus must have known that we would have such a difficult time with ourselves, trying to solve the problem of a selfish life. He uses the word *daily*. If we want to have victory over ourselves, our self-denial must be a *daily* part of us.

My wife's father says that every morning when he gets up, he repeats these words to his Lord: "I beseech you therefore, brethren, by the mercies of God, that ye present your bodies a living sacrifice, holy, acceptable, unto God, which is your reasonable service. And be not conformed to this world, but be ye transformed by the renewing of your minds, that you may prove what is that good and acceptable, and perfect will of God" (Rom. 12:1–2). After he quotes those two verses, he says, "Lord, I give you my eyes today so that I don't sin with them, and I give you my lips so that I don't say the wrong thing to somebody, and I give you my hands so that I don't do anything wrong. I give you my feet, Lord, so that I don't walk in the wrong place." He denies himself daily, every new morning. If you have a problem with self, may I suggest, deny yourself.

### *C. Matthew 10:24–39*

Third, Matthew 10:24–39. "A disciple is not above his teacher, nor a slave above his master. It is enough for the disciple that he become as his teacher and the slave as his master. If they have called the head of the house Beelzebul, how much more the members of the household. Therefore, do not fear them, for there is nothing covered that will not be revealed, and hidden that will not be known. What I tell you in the darkness, speak in the light; and what you hear whispered in your ear, proclaim upon the housetops. And do not fear those who kill the body, but are unable to kill the soul; but rather fear Him who is able to destroy both soul and body in hell. Are not two sparrows sold for a cent? And yet not one of them will fall to the ground apart from your Father. But the very hairs of your head are all numbered. Therefore, do not fear, you are of more value than many sparrows. Everyone therefore who shall confess Me before men, I will confess him before My Father who is in heaven. But whoever shall deny Me before men, I will also deny him before My Father who is in heaven. Do not think that I came to bring peace on the earth; I did not come to bring peace, but a sword. For I came to set a man against his father, and a daughter against her mother, and a daughter-in-law against her mother-in-law; and a man's enemies will be the members of his household. He who loves father and mother more than Me is not worthy of Me; and he who loves son or daughter more than Me is not worthy of Me. And he who does not take his cross and follow after me is not worthy of Me. He who has found his life shall lose it, and he who has lost his life for My sake shall find it."

Notice there are different circumstances. First, Jesus said that the servant is not greater than his lord. Second, he talked about their worries. They were worried about where their next meal was coming from, their next robe, and the shelter over their heads. He referred to the birds of the sky and said, "You are of more value than many sparrows." He talked about the family. A wife, husband, mother, father, daughter, or son can keep a Christian from following the Lord. Jesus said, "Regardless of what any member of your family does, that is no excuse for you to be unspiritual and un-Christlike. That is no excuse for you to exert your self-interest just because they stumble before you." If we let any member of our own family hinder us from serving Jesus, we are not worthy of Him.

*D. Matthew 16:24–27*

Fourth, Matthew 16:24–27. "Then Jesus said to His disciples, 'If anyone wishes to come after Me, let him deny himself, and take up his cross, and follow Me… For what will a man be profited, if he gains the whole world and forfeits his soul?" Some Christians forfeit the joys of the Christian life over something far smaller than the whole world.

One of the consequences of being selfish is that we sell short God's marvelous plan for us in exchange for a very small thing: a car, a boat, a house, a family member. We deny ourselves what God wants to give us: love, joy, and spiritual vitality because of something between us and Jesus because we want our own way.

Jesus added, "And He will recompense every man according to his deeds." Christians will give an account of all their deeds at the judgment seat. Therefore, is it not wise to avoid the selfish ones?

In summary, Jesus said, "Deny that self which exerts itself, so that Christ will be first, others second, and you last." He wants you to eat for He promised to provide for you. He wants you to sleep. He wants you to be healthy. He wants you to be strong. He wants you to be happy, to be at peace with yourself. But He wants you to do this His way, not your way.

Perhaps many of us are like the two little boys on a hobby horse.

One of them said to the other, "If only you would get off, I could ride much better." A young woman left a suicide note saying, "I am killing myself because I have never sincerely loved any human being all my life." Many people love in order to be loved in return. We treat others nicely because we know we will be treated kindly by them. We do not act out of sincerity. There is a big difference. Happiness is evasive. Try to grab it and it avoids you, but forget it and just give it without any thought of return, and God will flood you with it like an ocean wave.

John Calvin brought out this important truth when he said, "Even though we are degenerate and sinful men, still we are so constructed in the image of likeness of God that we will never be fulfilled in life, if left to our own selfish ends. That even in our depraved state, even in the light of our imperfection, we still cannot be satisfied and fulfilled in life, wanting our selfish desires. Even unsaved man feels better when he gives without any thought of return. How much, therefore, the Christian."

An elderly lady sat in the back of her chauffeur-driven car and went to the cemetery parking lot. She stayed in the car because she was too weak to walk. The chauffeur said to the cemetery manager, "Will you please speak to the lady because she is too weak to walk."

He went to her and she said to him, "I am the lady who has been mailing you the five dollars a week."

He said, "Oh yes, for the flowers."

She said, "Yes, for my husband's grave. I have just been told by my doctor that I only have a few more days to live. I don't care because I have nothing to live for. I want to make arrangements that five dollars a week will still be used for flowers on that grave."

He said, "Ma'am, it won't do that much good."

She was shocked.

Then he explained to her, "Please understand what I mean. I have been a member of a visiting society that goes to mental asylums and state hospitals. Those five dollars' worth of flowers would be so much better for people there who can see them, smell them, and feel them." She was totally taken aback. She ordered her chauffeur to drive away.

Two months later, the woman drove her own car to the cemetery office and walked up to the manager. With a bright happy smile, love beaming out, peace just bursting in her breast, she said, "You were so right two months ago. The reason I am still alive, the doctor does not know it, but I know it, is because I found a purpose for living. I did not send those flowers to hospitals and asylums, I brought them. And the joy I have found in bringing joy into other people's lives has given me a new purpose for living."

**Application**

Isn't that our purpose for living? If we could just stop seeking things for ourselves, and instead give to others what they need, we, too, would surprisingly find our happiness.

"But you, are you seeking great things for yourself?" asked the prophet Jeremiah (Jer. 45:5). "Do not seek them." Why? Because there is no greatness in things or in self-seeking people. But there is greatness in unselfish love, so seek that. As you do, be ever cautious that even self-denial can be a subtle form of self-seeking, and therefore nothing. So be cautious by double-checking that your motive for self-denial is selfless love.

Do you think this is not only difficult but perhaps impossible?

Perhaps you do not understand the true nature of love. Nothing is a hardship in love. Jesus said His yoke is easy and His load is light (Matt. 11:30). If you don't think His promise is true, perhaps it because you have not found Christ Himself! You must do what He says, "Come to me and I will give you rest." Do that right now and you will find the reality of this truth. Remember the words of Henry Drummond, “There is no happiness in having, or in getting, but only in giving.” Although the rest of the world is going in the wrong direction, we do not have to follow. Jesus in His sermon on the mount said, “It is more happy to give than to receive.”

# LIFE MESSAGE 8

## *Love Is Not Provoked*

The words of our Lord Jesus Christ from the Sermon on the Mount are equally fitting here at the beginning of this chapter as they were at the end of the previous chapter!

"You have heard that the ancients were told, 'You shall not commit murder,' and 'Whoever commits murder shall be liable to the court,' but I say to you that everyone who is angry with his brother shall be guilty…"

These are troublesome words to us because we all have a problem with anger, with getting provoked. Anger is a universal problem that has been around since the beginning of the world. That is why one of Adam's sons committed murder.

### I. The Character of Anger

"Love is not provoked." This truth in 1 Corinthians 13:5 rings in our ears as we hear the words of the first murderer echoing through the ages, "Am I my brother's keeper?" Cain's lying lips were attempting to cover up his fatal offense against his brother, Abel. What provoked Cain to murder his brother? Was it a momentary loss of composure, a fleeting fit of anger or rage, or was there an inward attitude that displayed itself in this moment of rage?

In Genesis 4:4–5, we have an answer to these searching questions.

Two brothers came before God with their offerings, "And the Lord had regard for Abel and for his offering; but for Cain and for his offering He had no regard." Why did God accept one offering and reject the other? God not only looks at the outward act but also at the inward heart attitude. God saw that Abel's heart was repentant before Him. He had a heart of love for God. But there was not true repentance in Cain's heart. He was not willing to humble himself before God in repentance. Cain's heart was selfish. Consequently, "Cain became very angry and his countenance fell." His anger manifested itself in the murder of his brother, Abel. An outward act cannot be divorced from an inward attitude. Anger is an inward attitude of the heart. Thus, the true character of anger is murder in the heart toward someone. Yes, we can get control of ourselves, so our anger does not go as far as murder. Nevertheless, murder is its true character. That is why Christ equated the two in Matthew 5:21–22.

Why is it that we can hear the story of Cain and Abel over and over again, and each time be horrified at the gross sin of murder, and yet hardly wink an eyelash at the inner attitudes that led up to this murder? Is it because we have excused anger as a weakness and say it is just our temperament? Can we excuse it that way? The Bible speaks about these inner sins of attitude just as much as it does about murder and adultery. Why does the Bible speak so much about them? Is it because we so readily tolerate them?

In Galatians 5:19–21, we read a list of sins, "Now the deeds of the flesh are evident, which are: immortality, impurity, sensuality, idolatry, sorcery, enmities, strife, jealousy, outbursts of anger, disputes, dissensions, factions, envyings, drunkenness, carousings and things like these." Strife, jealousy, outbursts of anger, disputes, dissensions, and factions are listed along with the worst carnal sins, and yet we treat them so lightly.

## II. The Cause of Anger

In his book *Spirit-Controlled Temperament*, Tim LaHaye wrote the following: "Although we love to excuse our weakness and justify them to ourselves as we nurse our grudges and indulge in angry, violated, bitter feelings, they are all motivated by selfishness. When I am angry, it is because someone has violated my rights and I am interested in myself. When I am bitter against someone, it is because they have done something against me, and again I come back to selfishness. Vengeance is always inspired by selfishness."

Observe a group of children playing at a playground, and it will not be long before you see selfishness and anger in action. Two little girls playing, the one yells, "It's my doll! I want to play with my doll. It's my turn!" Two little boys with a bat and ball, and one says, "It's my turn. I want the ball and bat now!"

The root cause of all these things boils down to one thing: selfishness. It is interesting that being provoked comes right after "love does not seek its own." This selfishness is not only evident in the lives of children but in the lives of adults as well. Husbands and wives often become angry with one another because they are more concerned with their own problems than they are with reaching out in love and sympathy toward their partner. When a husband comes home after a hard day's work, he is feeling tired and unaware that his wife had a hard day too. Each can be self-centered, so when they tell each other about their own problems, the other one thinks, "I had a harder day than her/him." We are selfish people. We think of ourselves. But love is not self-regarding. "Love is not provoked."

When we look at the basic cause of anger in all its forms: arguments, loss of temper, irritations, touchiness—it all boils down to selfishness.

## III. The Cost of Anger

What is the high price we pay for pent-up bitterness and anger stemming from selfishness? Paul writes in Ephesians 4:30–32, "And do not grieve the Holy Spirit of God, by whom you were sealed for the day of redemption. Let all bitterness and wrath and anger and clamor and slander be put away from you, just as God in Christ has also forgiven you."

Let us consider the high cost of anger in four areas: emotionally, socially, physically, and, most important of all, spiritually.

### *A. The Emotional Cost of Anger*

Suppressed anger and bitterness will cause tremendous emotional strain. We are designed by God to be intensely emotional creatures, but if we permit anger to dominate us, it will squelch the rich emotion of love.

Dr. S. I. McMillen, in his book *None of These Diseases*," makes an interesting statement about the emotional effects of anger: "The moment I start hating a man, I become his slave. I cannot enjoy my work anymore because he even controls my thoughts. My resentment produces too many stress hormones in my body and I become fatigued after only a few hours' work. The work I formerly enjoyed is now drudgery. Even vacations cease to give me pleasure…the man I hate hounds me wherever I go. I can't escape his tyrannical grasp on my mind. When the waiter serves me porterhouse steak with French fries, asparagus, crisp salad and strawberry shortcake smothered with ice cream, it might as well be stale bread and water. My teeth chew it and I swallow it, but the man I hate will not permit me to enjoy it...the man I hate may be many miles from my bedroom, but more cruel than a slave driver, he whips my thoughts into such a frenzy that my innerspring mattress becomes a rack of torture." What a price to pay for anger!

Anger takes many forms. Many people do not think they have a problem with anger. When Paul warned that "love is not provoked," he had in mind anger in all its variations. Consider the following to find out if you are an angry person: bitterness, malice, clamor, envy, resentment, intolerance, criticism, revenge, wrath, hatred, seduction, jealousy, attack, gossip, sarcasm, and unforgiveness. Several of these are in Ephesians chapter 4, and the rest of them are found in Paul's other writings. Many are under the misconception that only the one who shows a physical outburst is an angry person.

*B. The Social Cost of Anger*

The social price of anger and bitterness is exclusion from enjoyable times with other people. People do not want to be around an angry person. Many families have been torn apart, and many friendships have been ended by outworkings of anger. In Proverbs 22:24, there is this warning: "Do not associate with a man given to anger, or go with a hot-tempered man." The Bible warns "do not even associate with an angry person."

*C. The Physical Cost of Anger*

The physical cost of anger is also a financial cost. Anger and bitterness produce so much stress that often a person gets sick and spends much money for doctors to cure his problems. The physical problems are caused by inward anger. Doctors and medical associations say that from 60 to 90 percent of physical problems are emotionally induced. The majority of these sicknesses stem from either fear or anger. Because of the great physical cost, to yourself, beware of harboring anger.

*D. The Spiritual Cost of Anger*

We pay a high price in the spiritual realm for tolerating anger.

Anger grieves the Holy Spirit. Jesus Christ said, "I have come that you might have life and that you might have it more abundantly" (John 10:10). Abundant life can only be experienced when we are filled with the Holy Spirit. This cannot take place when we are grieving the Holy Spirit with our bitterness, wrath, anger, clamor, or malice.

If we grieve the Holy Spirit, we cannot expect to have the fruit of the Spirit in our lives. The presence of anger indicates the absence of love. If love is absent, we cannot experience peace, joy, patience, kindness, goodness, faithfulness, gentleness, and self-control.

## IV. The Correction of Anger

Having seen anger in its true character, and the high price we pay for it in every area of our lives, how we can correct it? How we can we stop grieving the Holy Spirit?

Paul writes in Philippians 2:5–8, "Have this attitude in yourselves which was also in Christ Jesus, who, although He existed in the form of God, did not regard equality with God, a thing to be grasped, but emptied Himself, taking the form of a bond-servant, and being made in the likeness of men. And being found in appearance as a man, He humbled Himself by becoming obedient to the point of death, even death on a cross."

Christ's attitude was one of meekness. Meekness is the opposite of anger. We get angry when someone infringes on our rights. Yet meekness means yielding personal rights to God. This is the only way to respond when we are tempted to get angry. This is the only way to correct anger—to give your rights to God, to humble yourself before God.

Look at the trial of Jesus Christ. He stood before Pontius Pilate, and the chief priests and elders accused Him falsely. He made no defense. He did not answer their charges. Pilate was amazed at Christ's attitude because the natural reaction would have been for Him to strike out in anger and self-defense.

They took Him away, they beat Him, they crowned Him with a crown of thorns, they mocked Him, they spit upon Him, and they nailed Him to a cross! What was his reaction? "Father, forgive them, for they know not what they do." For "love is not provoked," even to the point of death.

## Application

In applying this to yourself, you may have an objection similar to the following: You may feel that your outbursts of anger are part of being human and God understands. He knows you cannot be perfect, so you excuse yourself. However, anger can be the vice even of the best as well as of the worst people. Often, it is the one blemish on an otherwise excellent character. It is the one thing that can even make the best of people unappreciated. If we are angry, people tend to forget all the good we have done.

That may not seem fair, but that is the way it is. Mario Lanza was one of the greatest singers who ever lived, but he could offend people by his temper. We all know people who are so refined, except for their quick temper. They are easily offended and have short fuses. The striking compatibility of anger with high moral character is one of the strangest and saddest problems of ethics and religion.

No, none of us, no matter who we are, can afford to get provoked.

Let us be as diligent in getting rid of it as we are in dealing with what we think our worst sins may be.

# LIFE MESSAGE 9

## *Love Does Not Take into Account a Wrong Suffered*

Rudyard Kipling, in his great poem "If," wrote,

> If you can keep your head when all about you
> are losing theirs and blaming it on you.
> Or being lied about, don't deal in lies.
> Or being hated, don't give way to hating,
> Yours is the earth and everything that's in it,
> And which is more—you'll be a man, my son.

Perhaps you've heard these words before, but find they are hard to apply in your life. Perhaps you have often felt as the woman who poured out her problem to her pastor.

It seemed to be a very trivial matter, but as the counseling session progressed, the minister discerned that she was under great nervous stress. Her problem had begun years ago when she was living with her sister, an invalid. She ministered to her day after day, week after week, month after month, and year after year. She seemed to enjoy it, but deep down in her heart, she hated her sister. Although she tried to justify and explain away her feelings, this did not alleviate her suffering internally. The minister gave her some practical suggestions and then prescribed the only medicine that really could solve her problem: "You *must* forgive and forget."

## I. The Problem

Forgive and forget, we say. We can perhaps work ourselves up to forgiving a certain individual, but how can we forget? Years ago, a teacher of mine said, "Only God has the power to forget, not man. Man can forgive, but only God can forgive and forget." I raise the question, is that really true? Perhaps it is not, especially in light of the fact that so often our forgiveness seems so personally unsatisfying when we do not forget as well as forgive. But the real question is, how can you forget when the hurt is so deep? The answer is in 1 Corinthians 13:5: "Love is not provoked, love does not take into account a wrong suffered."

In the previous chapter, we discussed the fact that love is not provoked. There is an important connection between this and the subject of this chapter. We have to take the two together. There are two basic surface problems: Christians being provoked and Christians bearing resentment. But what is the relationship? Being provoked is the outward manifestation of anger. Many Christians do not show outward bursts of anger, but within them, they are keeping records of wrongs suffered from other people. These are both expressions of anger. Both find their root in the problem of anger. The person who does the latter hurts himself just as much as the person who does the former.

My father had a friend who, whenever he was provoked, blew his top. But once he did, he forgot about it; he had no resentment. He walked away, free from the ulcers of the problem.

But some people are like the magician on a ship going to Europe.

As he entertained the people with his tricks, a parrot belonging to one of the passengers said, "You're a faker!" The people applauded his tricks, but the parrot kept saying, "You're a faker!" This went on for some time, but the magician, of course, did not blow his top because he would lose the respect of his audience. He simply tried more fantastic tricks, trying to think of some way to get even with the parrot. Finally, as he attempted one last trick, the ship struck a mine and exploded. The magician and the parrot survived by clinging to a raft. The parrot studied the situation and then said, "OK, buddy, you win. But tell me, what did you do with the ship?"

When we allow resentment to build up, we lose the whole ship, so to speak. Benjamin Franklin once put it this way: "Doing an injury puts you below your enemy; revenging one makes you even with him; but forgiving the offense sets you above your enemy."

Keeping records of wrongs done is another way of expressing anger, just as much as getting provoked and blowing your top. Inside, we can become like a closed steam kettle. If it boils without any kind of release of steam, there's an explosion.

Not all twins are identical, even though they are born at the same time from the same parent. Being provoked and carrying resentment are not identical twins, but they come from the same parent—anger. Many people learn to control bursts of anger, but they keep records of wrongs done against them and they brood over those records. They read and reread those records until they make a mountain of hostility out of a molehill over some small offense. They get steamed up inside, even though they do not express it outwardly. That is resentment.

The word *resent* is an accounting term that means to mark down something like an item on a ledger so that it cannot be forgotten. That is exactly what we do when we are resentful. We mark down; we keep records. We take into account items—that is, the slights, injuries, offenses, harms, and wrongs that people do to us. On the surface, we may try to respond in a gracious manner, but inside we keep records, and this leads to a terrible problem. What is the solution?

## II. The Human Solution

There are two basic solutions: the human and the divine. First, the human.

### *A. Self-Justification (No Anger but No Forgiveness)*

There is the solution of self-justification. We justify ourselves by saying, "I did not get angry with that person." Think about the last time you had a conflict with some person and you walked away with a victory. "I didn't get provoked." But in your heart, you harbored the wrong. You did not forget. There is something there on the ledger of your heart toward that person. You justify yourself because you did not blow your top and get angry. Is that really a solution? Such a human solution, although it is practiced by many Christians, is very inadequate.

### *B. Self-Rationalization (Forgiving but Not Forgetting)*

The other human solution is self-rationalization. This is saying, "Well, I'll forgive him, but how could I ever forget?" That attitude is very common. Perhaps you have resigned yourself to that solution, so far as getting along with your husband, wife, parent, child, or friend is concerned. Is that really the solution God wants us to practice? No, God has a better way in store for us. Some clues to this better way are found in these quotations:

> What a grand world this would be if we could forget our troubles as easily as we forget our blessings.

Is it hard to forget when we were wronged? We do not seem to have a problem forgetting our blessings. Why can't we forget our wrongs just as easily as we forget our blessings? Another,

> Always remember to forget the things that made you sad, but never forget to remember the things that made you glad.

That is a good one to memorize. Also,

> If you were busy being true to what you knew you ought to do, you'd be so busy, you'd forget the blunders of the folks you met.

**III. The Divine Solution**

This leads to the divine solution. God has the real answer for us.

To help you remember and apply God's way, write these three lines on one side of a 3 × 5 card:

- Forgive and forget.
- Forgive without regret.
- Forgive to beget.

If you do your forgiving that way, there will be an exciting change in your life. You will be clean and free with other people. Forgive and forget; forgive without regret; forgive to beget. We will consider them in that order.

### *A. Forgive and Forget*

In Psalms 103:11, we read, "For high as the heavens are above the earth, so great is His loving kindness toward those who fear Him. As far as the east is from the west, so far has He removed our transgressions from us." This is God's way of forgiving. He moves our sins from Himself as far as the east is from the west. He forgets as well as forgives. This is the pattern for us.

Isaiah 43:25 declares, "I, even I, am the one who wipes out your transgressions for My own sake; and I will not remember your sins." That is beautiful! And the very next words are "Put Me in remembrance." If we are busy remembering the Lord, we will have no problem forgetting other people's sins against us.

In Jeremiah 31:34, we read, "And they shall not teach again, each man his neighbor and each man his brother, saying 'Know the Lord,' for they shall all know Me from the least of them to the greatest of them, declares the Lord, for I will forgive their iniquity, and their sin I will remember no more." We must not only agree with this teaching about God's forgiveness but must do it ourselves. We are to be like God in His forgiveness. He is our Heavenly Father, and we are His children. Therefore, we are to resemble him in His character.

Then there is the command of Ephesians 4:32: "And be kind to one another, tender-hearted, forgiving each other, just as God in Christ also has forgiven you." Just as God forgives and forgets, so should we. We cannot escape it; we are committed to it; there is no other way.

If we find this command difficult to obey, we can find help in the second part of God's three-fold solution: forgive without regret.

### *B. Forgive without Regret*

Why do we not want to forget so many times? Because we are afraid that if we do not remember, we may be wronged again. Another reason why we remember instead of forgetting is because we think the person who wronged us has not had chastisement from us. We want him to feel how hurt we really are. We cannot face the fact that he may go scot-free, so we do not give up our regrets.

We must learn instead to leave that person in the hands of the Lord.

First Peter 4:8 tells us how to do it. "Above all, keep fervent in your love for one another, because love covers n multitude of sins." If we do not forgive without regrets, our love cannot cover even one sin, let alone a multitude of them. When we cover something the way God means it here, you cannot see it—it is almost as if it's not there. This kind of love means giving no room to feeling sorry for yourself.

James 5:20 says, "Let him know that he who turns a sinner from the error of his way will save his soul from death, and will cover a multitude of sins." Peter says that by loving him, we will cover a multitude of sins. James says we can actually turn him away. When a person who has wronged you feels that you have forgiven him freely without personal regrets, he opens up to you and receives your corrections by your example. You can turn him from his sin by the way you respond to him, by forgiving without regrets. You can be the instrument that God uses to turn him to Himself and away from a multitude of sins. This is why wives, in 1 Peter 3:1, are commanded to win their unsaved husbands by the power of their deeds and attitudes.

*C. Forgive to Beget*

The third part of God's three-fold solution is to forgive to beget.

Forgive to beget what? First, forgive to beget the confidence that you are forgiven by God.

1. The Confidence That You Are Forgiven by God

Let that flow into you; let that saturate into your consciousness. If we find it hard to keep from being resentful, it is perhaps because we have not fully accepted forgiveness by God. As the "Lord's Prayer" directs us, we are in a position to forgive because God has forgiven us. No one can really forgive another unless he has been forgiven by God Himself. His forgiveness gives us the capacity to forgive and forget. If you make it your intent to forgive to the point of forgetting, it gives you renewed confidence in and appreciation for God's forgiveness.

2. The Influence on Others to Forgive Like You

Second, forgive to beget the influence that you can have on other people to forgive and forget also. Do not be an island to yourself. Do not be so selfish that you think you live unto yourself. The way that you forgive and forget will encourage and influence others to forgive and forget in like manner.

In that great drama *Quo Vadis*, we are told of Chilo and Raucus.

Chilo was a very wicked man, the right-hand man of the Roman emperor Nero. So loyal was he to Nero that when his good friend Raucus became a Christian, Chilo thought nothing of selling his friend's wife and children into slavery. He betrayed Raucus to the Roman soldiers, who tortured him and put him to the stake to be burned. Raucus was asked to deny his faith and to recant his position, but he did not. And so he was burned alive. Nero, with Chilo by his side, went down the long line of people being burned alive. They finally came to the stake on which Raucus was burning. As they looked at the human torch that was Raucus, the wind blew the smoke away from his head. Chilo looked and saw him. He was struck in his conscience with a horrible sense of guilt. Caught up in the pain of such guilt, he cried, "Raucus, will you please forgive me?" He saw Raucus' head near the top of the stake tilt a little bit. Then came the words with a groan, "I forgive," and his head fell. Chilo was cut to the heart. With a beam of light in his face, he turned to Nero and said, "You are the wrong one!" Within an hour or so, Chilo found himself in the midst of a crowd of Christians. Among them was also the Apostle Paul. Paul said to him, "Oh, the truths of infinite forgiveness!" Chilo believed them and was baptized on the spot. The next day, he, too, was seized by the Roman officials and he, too, was asked to recant his faith, but he would not. But Chilo asked, "May I please die the same way the Christians did, especially Raucus?" They bound him to the stake and jabbed him with iron bars. But while they were doing so, he kissed the hands of those who were binding him. With a look of love, he said to all of them, "I forgive you, for you don't know what you're doing." He was put on the stake, the stake was lifted up, and he was burned alive.

**Application**

Chilo did it because he had been forgiven. He did it because he learned to forgive. His Christian faith gave him the power to forgive and forget. Love means to forgive and forget. Love is not resentful. Love does not keep records of wrongs suffered.

Now take your 3 × 5 card, and on the other side write the names of people whom you must go to and forgive, with the intention of forgetting their wrongs as well. Write on your card "Love forgives and forgets." Now ask God for the power to forget as well as to forgive.

Perhaps there are two or three people whose offenses you have not forgotten. Be honest with yourself and with God. What good is truth about love unless it is practiced. Perhaps there is something that you have done wrong yourself, for which you have not forgiven yourself—that's very common among Christians. God wants you to forget the sins He has already forgiven in Christ. Perhaps some of your own unforgotten sins should be on your list. Right now you can ask God for the power to forget as well as to forgive.

# LIFE MESSAGE 10

## *Love Does Not Rejoice in Unrighteousness*

Clarence Macartney's mother told him many moral tales that made striking impressions on him that he carried through life. One of them was about the army general stationed in India who had a pet tiger cub. He was a very affectionate tiger, just like a little kitten. As the days, months, and years went by, the tiger became strong, full in strength and stature.

One day the general was doing some research in his study and fell asleep at his desk. His tiger was so affectionate, even when full grown, that he started to lick the general's hand as it dangled from the desk. There was a slight cut on his hand, and the tiger licked it. Before long, having licked the scab clean, the tiger liked the taste of blood. Suddenly, the once little, tiny playful cub became a wild beast. The next thing the general knew the tiger was on top of him. He awakened and looked into the eyes, not of his pet, but of a raging beast ready to devour him. Just in time, he grabbed his pistol and shot the tiger.

In the moral realm, the story never ceased to influence Macartney's conduct through life. He compared it to making pets of "affectionate sins" that perhaps seem totally harmless, sins we cuddle, enjoy, and play around with, so to speak. Macartney knew such pets would grow to be raging beasts that would one day require his life.

Something like this is in the Apostle Paul's mind in 1 Corinthians 13:6, where he writes, "Love does not rejoice in unrighteousness, but rejoices with the truth." That is the literal translation of the passage. Traditionally we have been taught that this verse means that we should not be happy with wickedness itself, as an abstract thing in life. As we shall see, however, the meaning is far deeper. Love goes beyond that.

We want to make three observations about love in this verse: love do not rejoice in unrighteousness 1) because love knows the deceitfulness of sin, 2) because love grieves over sin, and 3) because love hates sin.

## I. Because Love Knows the Deceitfulness of Sin

### *A. Defining Not Rejoicing in Unrighteousness*

How can love know sin's deceitfulness? Try to imagine what it means not to rejoice over some unrighteousness. No doubt it means that we should not be happy when we hear about something going wrong with a friend, even if that friend somehow offended us and we were tempted to rejoice over the fact that God is getting even with him for our sake. It also means that we should not rejoice over what happens to our enemies, our own and our country's.

Going a bit deeper, it means we should not be happy when we get a report about some friend or some foe who has fallen into some fault mistake or sin. But, more deeply, it also means we should not take pleasure in what we may think are secret sins. We should not rejoice in such unrighteousness.

Love does not rejoice over the vices of other men, does not take delight when they are guilty of crime, or when in any matter they fall into sin. It does not find pleasure in hearing others accused of sin and in having it proved that they committed it. Love does not find malicious pleasure in the report that they have done wrong, or in following up that report and having it established.

Perhaps you have heard of the little boy's prayer. He was taught by his mommy to pray and ask God to take away his sins, those "naughty things" as she called them. So he said, "Dear God, please take away the naughty things I did today. But, dear Father, in case you don't, I won't mind because I enjoy them anyhow." He was being very sincere and honest as children are. He really meant it. He spoke the way many Christians feel because of their own self-deception.

*B. Departmentalizing Such Rejoicing*

Yes, we must admit certain sins we take pleasure in. We can begin to change our lives, however. Begin by looking at the Word of God. Romans 1:32 shows the logical conclusion of the tolerance of sin in our lives. "And although they know the ordinance of God, that those who practice such things are worthy of death, they not only do the same, but also give hearty approval to those who practice them." *Them* refers to all the sins of the flesh that are listed in verses prior to verse 32.

Christians, of course, are not in the category of being condemned by God to hell. However, human nature in the Christian is the same as human nature in the non-Christian. Although the believer has a new nature in Christ Jesus, there is still the potential of the old self exerting itself, just like the general's pet tiger. That "tiger" of self will linger until the day we die and go to heaven. Potentially it is ready at any point to devour us, if we let it. Therefore, there is the potential within us to do whatever sins the world does, if we don't watch and keep a check on that old beast in us day by day. This means that we must bear our cross and deny ourself, until we meet Jesus face to face.

In Romans 12:1–2, we are commanded by Paul, "I urge you therefore, brethren, by the mercies of God, to present your bodies a living and holy sacrifice, acceptable to God, which is your spiritual service of worship. And do not be conformed to this world (Why would God have to command us not to be like the sinners in the world unless He knew we had the potential to be like that, Christians or not?) but be transformed by the renewing of your mind, that you may prove what the will of God is, that which is good and acceptable and perfect."

All of you reading this book have the potential to murder, we all have the potential to lie, cheat, steal, to commit adultery, and to break the commands of God. That is why St. Augustine said, in such fitting words, "The Christian has the potential to do the very sin he watched his brother do, apart from the grace of God." Beware, the scripture says, let him who stands take heed lest he fall.

*C. Discerning Such Rejoicing*

There is another dimension to this matter of rejoicing over evil or unrighteousness. What happens to you when you actually take pleasure in the sin, mistake, or fault of someone else or yourself? Does it not encourage you to do it again? Does it not make you go in the opposite direction to which Christ has called you? Does not it make you sow to the flesh, and therefore reap more to the flesh? Yes, a person who rejoices in unrighteousness is affected in three ways.

1. In Terms of Pride

When we hear about someone falling short in something, especially someone we do not like or who has offended us, we have a certain sense of pride that we are at least as good as he is, if not better. That feeds our ego. What does the Bible say about that? Look at Proverbs 6:16: "There are six things which the Lord hates, yes, seven which are an abomination to him: Haughty eyes (eyes that are just looking for things that can feed pride), a lying tongue and hands that shed innocent blood, a heart which devises wicked plans, feet that run rapidly to evil, a false witness who utters lies and one who spreads strife among brothers." I want to focus on "a heart that devises wicked plans." A person who rejoices in unrighteousness is devising wickedness in his heart. Love does not do that.

In Proverbs 15:25, we read, "The Lord will tear down the house of the proud, but He will establish the boundary of the widow." If we rejoice over evil, it is because we are proud. If we are proud, we can be sure that God will tear us down because God resists the proud and gives grace to the humble.

2. In Terms of Selfishness

What else happens to me when I am rejoicing over unrighteousness? What else would cause me to smile to a wife, husband, or friend when another person goes wrong? It is selfishness. First Corinthians 13:5 says, "Love does not act unbecomingly." Love does not seek its own. But whenever we take pleasure in the failings of another, is that not exactly what we are doing? We are seeking to satisfy, gratify, and fulfill our own ego, ourselves.

3. In Terms of Hate

The third thing that causes us to rejoice in unrighteousness is hatred. Since love does not do this sort of thing, then what does? There's only one alternative: hate. Outwardly, you do not hate the person. You are not emotionally angry with that person; you do not have any kind of violence toward him. But that does not mean that you do not hate him. Hatred really is the absence of love. Love is absent when we get pleasure over somebody's sin. Therefore, we hate that person. It is said of Moses that he chose to suffer with the people of God, rather than to enjoy the pleasures of sin for a season. There is lots of pleasure in staying home from church when you should be at the Lord's house. There is a lot of pleasure in transgressing against the laws of God, but that does not make it right. Enjoying such pleasures that make you deviate from the ways of Christ is really self-hatred. It makes you go against what God has created you to be in all your fullness. Put a frog into a pot of hot water and he will jump right out again.

But put that same frog into a pot of cool water, and he'll stay there. Turn on the stove and let the water get warm, and the frog will stay there. He will endure the gradually rising temperature, hotter water than he would if he were dropped into it. He will stay there long enough to get boiled. Many Christians are like that. They are not aware of the degree of temperature that the sin in their life produces. They are so comfortable that they are engulfed in the pleasure of sin. They do not know when to get out. The little boy walked down the church aisle with his class, followed by his teacher. He got into trouble by tripping on a few choir robes. He got in the way of a few people and really acted up in general. But he had his alibi: "The devil was so fast, he got me to do wrong before I knew it." Not really! The boy did certain things with great pleasure before that point, and then he did more overt acts. The devil was not fast. The boy was slow. That is the truth about us too.

## II. Because Love Grieves over Sin

Love grieving over sin? Yes, love does not rejoice over evil because it grieves over sin. This is foreign to us because so many of us are too close to sin in our lives, we do not want to grieve over it. We do not even feel the necessity of grieving over it.

First of all, the word *grief* means regret or disappointment or great disheartenment over something. That is, when you hear the report of someone who gets fouled up in sin, perhaps even an enemy or yourself, rather than taking pleasure in it, love does just the opposite. Love grieves over the stumbling. That is what love does for us. If we practiced that response to sin, we would not keep on practicing the sin. If we practiced grieving over whatever sin we commit, or someone else commits, we would not have the problems that we ourselves have with other people. We need to learn how to grieve.

There once was a country newspaper editor who got tired of being told he was biased in his news reports. Some of his disgruntled subscribers charged him with being a liar. In angry retort, he announced that in the following week's paper, he would tell the full truth about everybody and everything. As human nature is, they were looking forward to it. But he outguessed them. When it came off the press, this is what the villagers found: "Dave Conkey died at his home last Friday evening, and there was a big funeral Sunday afternoon. The minister said it was a loss to the community, but I doubt it. The community is better off without him. The doctor said he died of a heart attack; nonsense, whiskey killed him. The Wednesday Literary Club met in the home of Mrs. Gadabout. The program stated that they were going to study Shakespeare's play *Much Ado about Nothing*. Well, they did not. The lady who was assigned to present the paper had never read the play, and so they had no program. But they made up for it by gossiping about every member who wasn't there, and the whole afternoon was really like the play *Much Ado about Nothing*.

"Winifred Jones and Jim Smith were married Saturday afternoon at the Methodist parsonage. The bride is a very ordinary girl who does not know any more about cooking than a jack rabbit and never helped her mother three days in her life. She is not a beauty by any means and has a gait like a duck. The groom is an up-to-date loafer. He spends most of his time hanging around a pool hall. He has been living off his old folks at home all his life and is not worth shucks. It will be a hard life for both of them."

We get the point, don't we? People like to hear the truth so long as it is about someone else. But how we fear the truth being told about ourselves. Love is so grieved over the sin of someone else, it produces compassion toward that person, even though the sin itself is not accepted.

Chrysostom, the great early church father, was arrested by the Roman emperor for his faith. In the court hall, the Romans maliciously were involved in figuring out what kind of torture to administer. The emperor turned to his counselors and said, "What shall we do with him? Shall we put him in the dungeon?"

The counselors said, "No, because he would love, he would enjoy, he would have pleasure in being in solitude like that in which he could meditate upon his God. We cannot put him in a dungeon." The emperor said, "Shall we put him on a stake and kill him?" The answers from the counselors came again, "No, he would love to die because he knows that when he dies, he will be with the presence of his Heavenly Father forever. We can't even give him death."

"Then what shall we do?" said the emperor.

This is what they said: "If you want to make Chrysostom pain, cause Chrysostom to sin. That's what makes him pain."

Would it not be wonderful if each of us were so Christlike that we could think the same way? Practice grieving over sin and that will be your attitude too.

Love also hates sin. Love does not rejoice in unrighteousness because love hates sin. In Zachariah 8:16–17, we read, "These are things which you should do: Speak the truth to one another; judge with truth and judgment for peace in your gates. Also let none of you devise evil in your heart against another, and do not love perjury; for all these things are what I hate, declares the Lord."

The word *perjury* means dishonesty, bearing false witness. This is what some people do when the preacher calls on them to find out why they are persisting in their sin. They must think preachers are stupid because of all the excuses they give for why they are not doing what they should be doing.

In Psalm 5:4, we read, "For thou art not a God that takes pleasure in wickedness." That's why love does not rejoice and take pleasure in wickedness because God does not. God is love. God, who is rich in love, mercy, and grace, does not take pleasure in wickedness. He will not coddle you in yours, either. He is not that loving; that would be a denial of what He is. "No evil dwells with Thee. The boastful shall not stand before Thine eyes: Thou dost hate all those who do iniquity." That upsets the applecart of those who think God hates the sin but loves the sinner.

In Psalm 45:7, we read, "Thou hast loved righteousness and hated wickedness." God loves the one and hates the other. Speaking of the Lord Jesus, Hebrews 1:9 says, "Thou hast loved righteousness and hated lawlessness." Revelation 2:6: "Yet this you do have, that you hate the deeds of tile Nicolatians, which I also hate." Not only does God hate sin, but He also commends believers who hate sin. Do you hate sin? Do you hate the sin of other people because it makes you grieve over them, instead of having pleasure in it? Do you hate your own sin so much that you are broken over it, or do you persist in having pleasure in doing wrong and then excusing yourself for it?

### III. Application in Paul

In Romans chapter 7, we find a portrait of the Apostle Paul. In verse 15, he writes, "For that which I am doing, I do not understand; for I am practicing what I would like to do, but I am doing the very thing I hate." Paul learned to hate sin, but that in itself did not make him stop doing it, did it?

Note verse 16: "But if the very thing I do, I do not wish to do, I agree with the law, confessing that it is good. So now, no longer am I the one doing it, but sin which dwells within me. For I know that nothing good dwells in me, that is my flesh; for the wishing is present in me, but the doing of good is not. For the good that I wish, I do not do; but I practice the very evil that I do not Wish. But if I am doing the very thing I do not wish, I am no longer the one doing it, but sin which dwells in me. I find then the principle that evil is present in me, the one who wishes to do good. For I joyfully concur with the law of God in the inner man."

He adds in verse 24, "Wretched man that I am!" That is one of the most godly things you can do, frustrated over your sin, if you go on to ask, "Who will set me free from the body of this death? Thanks be to God through Jesus Christ our Lord!" Do you have that feeling toward a neighbor or brother? It is been well said, "The biggest trouble with sin is the 'I' in the middle of the word."

Henry Ward Beecher made a very interesting comment when he said, "For every hundred preachers that are hacking away at the branches of sin, there is at best only one preacher hacking away at the root of it." I trust we have hacked away at the root. For every hundred preachers who hack away at the branches, there are a thousand average Christians playing around with the fruit of sin and having pleasure in it. Let us get to the root, shall we? Let us learn to avoid pleasure in sin.

## Application

In his powerful short story "The Minister's Black Veil," Nathaniel Hawthorne portrays the time when a church in New England had a minister come to the congregation. Everybody was excited. They had been many months without a preacher. Finally, came the morning in which the new preacher walked into the pulpit. But to the amazement of everyone, he walked in wearing a black veil. The people looked and wondered. Some conjectured that he had a diseased face and was covering it up so as not to offend the people.

Others thought he was in bereavement because of the loss of a loved one. Others went a step further and said he was using the veil as a symbol of his own penitence over some sin he had done. But the thing really remained secret. The preacher did not reveal that day why he was wearing it. Weeks, months, years went by; finally his entire ministry was there. Every Sunday and every day, the minister wore the black veil. Wherever he went, he wore it, until finally one day, he grew ill and was found dying. A neighboring preacher went to his home and inquired, "What is the secret behind the black veil? Please tell me so you don't go to your grave taking the secret down into it with you." With his dying strength, the preacher with the black veil sat up in bed and turned to the other preacher and said, "Why are you so concerned about my black veil. Oh, how men have avoided me. Oh, how women have shunned from pitying me. Oh, how children have creamed and run from me, all the years of my ministry because of this little piece of cloth, when in their own lives, they have a black veil behind which they treasure their own pleasure in sins, secret sins and never change. Don't worry about my black veil," said the preacher to the neighboring preacher. "Worry about you and your people's veils."

What about yours? What kind of black veil are you hiding behind? Love takes no pleasure, even in the secret sins behind your black veil.

# LIFE MESSAGE 11

## *Love Rejoices the Truth*

It was a wintry Christmas morning. The family gathered inside the house was not very happy. The mother was dead; a wayward son was not yet home. His sisters and brothers were gathered around the tree. Finally their brother walked in. He had been out all night drinking. He walked in rather ashamed because it was Christmas morning. It was the last straw for his sisters and brothers, and they pressured their father to put him out. As the day progressed, the father came to the conclusion that he must appeal to his family. After a long discussion, the vote was unanimous; expulsion was the only solution. So the father turned to the boy, and there in that little home in Manchester, England, the young lad heard the words, "Your sisters and brothers have unanimously voted that you be expelled from our house. You have been coaxed. You have been threatened. You have been punished, and you just refuse to change. They have asked you to leave and yet, my son, I love you. I believe in you. Yes, in spite of all the things you have done wrong, I believe the potential within you, and for that reason, I cannot let you go." Hearing such words of love and confidence, the boy broke into tears. His soul melted. He experienced for the first time the living Jesus Christ. That boy became none other than the great Henry Morehouse of Manchester, one of the greatest preachers who has ever lived.

Such a story helps us to understand the truth of 1 Corinthians 13:6: "Love does not rejoice in unrighteousness but rejoices with the truth." The father of that young man rejoiced in the truth of the potential in his life, even when everything else looked dark.

How many Christians could really be like that? For so many, when someone rubs us the wrong way, especially in our families, we get irritated and hurt. We miss a traffic light and lose our peace. We get behind schedule and become irritated toward our loved ones. We know so little about rejoicing in truth. As parents, we quickly get impatient with our children, especially when they are trying to do something right and they cannot do it. We jump on them and forget to rejoice in the truth of their attempt and potential. We men so often criticize our wives for what they do wrong, but we do not rejoice about what they do right. Wives many times nag their husbands and do not rejoice in their accomplishments. One reason we do not win more souls to the Lord is because we do so little rejoicing in the lives of others, rejoicing in the truth that is in them, even though they are unbelievers.

Love rejoicing in the truth introduces the whole matter of what a truly positive personality is like. There are three categories of personalities: 1) the minus personality, 2) the middle-of-the-road personality, and 3) the marvelous personality. There are three types of personality, but only one type fits the words of 1 Corinthians 13:6: "Love rejoices with and in the truth." In order to appreciate that truth, we have to see by contrast what the alternatives are.

## I. The Minus Personality

Consider the minus personality. As you do, be honest and ask yourself, am I like this one, or am I more like this one, or am I like the third?

### *A. His Career*

The minus personality makes a career of emphasizing the faults of people, that is picking them to pieces. This is his lifestyle.

### *B. His Contagion*

Such a personality is contagious. This is because so often we as human beings are so much more alert and curious about hearing negative things. We like to hear minus things instead of plus things—things that tear people down instead of build them up. Such influence spreads much faster than good influence does. A minus person is very good at this: "Did you know? I don't mean to gossip but…" "I don't mean to be a backbiter, but did you know?" "I haven't told him this because I'm not really sure it's right, but did you know?" "I wouldn't go to him because it would hurt his feeling, but guess what he did the other day?" These are typical of how the minus person talks. Unfortunately, he sets off a chain reaction that spreads to many other people.

### *C. His Commonplace*

The minus personality has a career, he is contagious, and he has a commonplace about himself. The reason so many of us respond to hearing negative things about other people; the reason we sit around and talk about other people; the reason why we have "roast preacher" for dinner on Sunday is because by nature we have a gravitational pull toward the nature of a minus personality. We all have this minus potential within us. We all realize that going downhill is much easier than going uphill. Even though we know it is wrong, we continue.

During the days of Lincoln, a man went to such an extreme that he even criticized Lincoln for making friends out of his enemies. He said, "I thought you were to treat your enemies by destroying them, not by kindness and love and thoughtfulness and other virtues."

Lincoln replied, "By making friends out of my enemies, have I not destroyed my enemies?" The minus person destroys even the good that a positive person would do. Barnes says, "Minus people are people who rejoice in the vices instead of the virtues of others." But a truly loving person rejoices not in the vices but in the virtues of people.

## II. The Middle-of-the-Road Personality

By definition, the middle-of-the-road personality does not really tear down people because after all, that is not nice, but on the other hand, he does not really build up people either. He is just a person who does not want to get involved. He shies away from anything that looks like an issue. He is a middle-of-the-roader. He has a way of playing it safe, of being noncontroversial.

### *A. Danger*

Unfortunately, however, there is a very great danger in this kind of a personality. Such a person usually compromises truth because of his tendency toward false love. I was eating lunch with the township manager, and he brought out something that

I have felt for a long time but could not verbalize because of my lack of experience. He said, "I get so upset with people, Christians especially, who think love is always namby-pamby, that love doesn't preserve and protect truth, and rejoice in truth. Rejoicing in truth doesn't always mean being kind and gracious, but it may mean standing up for the truth, and calling a spade a spade, and letting a person know when he is wrong, not to tear him down, but to let him know where he's wrong to build him up. That's also rejoicing in truth." How important that is. So many of us under the guise of love, overlook wrongs in others. We quote the verse, "Love covers a multitude of sins," without understanding what it means. It really means to go to a person and expose his sin in love, spiritually, meekly, with lowliness, with the intent of building him up, and getting him beyond it. That is how you cover the multitude of sins. If he repents of it, you will save him from a multitude of sins after that. That's what it means for love to cover a multitude of sins. The great danger for a middle-of-the-road Christian is to compromise the truth. Such a middle-of-the-roader was Lot.

*B. Description*

Go back to the time when Abraham and Lot split because their servants could not get along. Lot, the aggressive, young, ambitious man, chose the plains of Sodom and Gomorrah. He thought it was a land of promise. Abraham took whatever was left. Lot lived right there in Sodom. But first he pitched his tent toward the city, and then he lived in it. Down he went. He was a real believer because the Bible calls him righteous. But what happened? He certainly did not want to insult anybody in Sodom. Out of compromise, he overlooked their homosexuality, their beastly way of living. He compromised truth so he became of no use to God. But he was so far from the world that he was no use to the world either. He was in the miserable middle of the road. He escaped by the very skin of his teeth when judgment came to Sodom and Gomorrah. His wife looked back, and he lost her for she became a pillar of salt. His daughters committed adultery with him. That was the cost of Lot's middle-of-the-road position. We must count the cost of continuing in a middle-of-the-road Christianity.

*C. Doom*

Such a middle-of-the-road life leads to doom. If a car goes down the middle of the road, one of three things will happen: 1) it will go be backward, especially with oncoming traffic coming around the curve; 2) it will break right down; or 3) it will boom right into a collision. Staying in the middle of the road requires so much effort that it's like going uphill in the Christian life. You wind up just going backward. The "engine" of the Christian life cannot take such pressure. It breaks down because your life is constantly involved in not tearing people down or building them up, not making any kind of personal contribution to anybody. Life becomes a series of "flats" and emptiness, like being in the desert and breaking down, without water. Being in the middle is a collision course because you are headed for a collision with the condemnation of God. In Ephesians 5:11, Paul says something about the middle-of-the-road Christian, the person who does not want to get involved, who wants to be neutral about everything, "and do not participate in the unfruitful deeds of darkness." If we say nothing about sin, we have participated in it. It's only a matter of time before your life becomes equivalent to it. The solution is spelled out, "but instead even expose them." Love that rejoices in the truth and with the truth does not circumvent and detour around that responsibility. We are to expose the evil works of darkness.

In Proverbs 28:13, we read, "He who conceals his transgressions will not prosper." This person will break down, he will fail, he will never reach his destination. "But he who confesses and forsakes them will find compassion."

Consider Proverbs 17:15, to paraphrase it: "He who justifies the wicked is also one who winds up criticizing the righteous, and because of such receives the condemnation of God." That verse makes it clear that the person who tries to be in the middle of the road by overlooking or justifying wrong will also attack the person who does right. In doing so, he is under the condemnation of God. Some Christians are so tolerant of unsaved people, of wicked people, and of sinning Christians, and yet they can get angry at a Christian who does right. This is because being in the middle of the road is an impossible situation. Such people criticize the righteous and live like the unrighteous. They will experience the condemnation of God. This is a more devastating type than the minus personality, but it is more common among Christians. The majority of Christians fall into the middle category, not being too hot for Christ or too cold.

## III. The Marvelous Personality

Now we must move on to the marvelous personality. Marvelous personality? Does that not sound farfetched? Yes, you can actually be a marvelous person. Let us define it first.

### *A. He Is the Plus Personality*

He is a plus person. If the minus person tears down, the plus person builds up. If the minus person criticizes and picks to pieces, the marvelous person, or the plus person, puts people together and adds to their lives. He knows how to encourage.

He not only sees where a person is wrong, he encourages him how to do it right.

"What I need most," wrote Emerson, "is something to make me do what I can." One of the most rewarding experiences you can ever have is to be that something for someone, to be the catalyst that dispels inertia and brings out the best in someone you know.

The thing that brings out the best in people is encouragement.

No matter what your circumstances are, you can provide those around you with precious morale plasma. Think encouraging thoughts, speak encouraging words, and, most important of all, adopt an air of confident expectancy toward those you are trying to help. Be genuinely interested; let your attitude be more eloquent that your words. In this way, you can be a *best friend*. There is no rejoicing quite comparable to the rejoicing you can earn in this way.

The plus personality is one who encourages. It is finding out what a person needs. It is finding good in him, to give him the courage to get over the difficulties. Are you minus, middle of the road, or plus? Did you open this book with a suspicious attitude to find out what you could find wrong with somebody? Do you sit there with the attitude "Now I'll sit down and read this book to see how he tries to bless me. I dare him to bless me!" Or did you open the book with an expectation of God's blessing you as you read it? Did you feel like you were going to put your best effort to your reading? Can you test your spirit right now? Is your spirit right now that old minus or middle of the road? Do you want a plus spirit? Would you move in that direction?

*B. Every Human Heart Yearns for This Treatment*

Think of Jesus. He believed in a Samaritan half-breed and gave her the way to eternal life, the kind of life that can destroy all the racial, marital, social, and political strife between people. Jesus Christ believed in a Roman soldier. Although he was not a Jew, yet his deeds of kindness shamed those who would dare name the name of God. Jesus saw even in a prostitute the potential of a powerful love. She came to love Him so much that she washed His feet with her tears. He saw the potential of latent stability and greatness in Peter, a very impetuous and impulsive man. He was not rated very high on the scale of successful people. He was a minus personality. We would not have chosen him to be the leader of the Apostles. But Jesus saw the potential, and He brought it out. He did not tear him down. Every human heart needs and yearns for that kind of love from somebody. All of us want people to look for and find the potential in us.

John Short had it right when he talked about little children: "Even little children bloom in the sunshine that is of the spirit that encourages and helps them whenever they try to do well. There is a child in every heart." He tells of the Scottish preacher who long years ago died and of whom it was said, "There is no one left in our village to appreciate the triumphs of ordinary folks." That tells all that we need to know about him. He truly understood the spirit of the Master, a spirit which our world needs so desperately, for there is so much bitterness, hatred, and suspicion in our time.

Who of us needs a reminder of more importance than this, namely that love is always so eager to believe the best, that love is never glad when others go wrong, that love is only gladdened by goodness? Yes, a truly positive personality is one who underscores the best in every man.

C. Even the Demon-Possessed Turn On

Even a possessed man with a legion of demons responded to that kind of love. "And as He was getting into the boat, the man who had been demon-possessed was entreating Him that he might accompany Him. And He did not let him, but He said to him, 'Go home to your people and report to them what great things the Lord has done for you, and how He had mercy on you.' And he went off and began to proclaim in Decapolis what great things Jesus had done for him; and everyone marvelled" (Mark 5:18–20).

May I tell you two reasons why they marvelled? One because of his absolute change. The man was demon-possessed, and he was delivered of his demons, he was a new man, no longer a raging, beast-like individual. That would make anybody marvel. Second, he must have tasted of such love from the Master that when he went back to that town, there was not a person who felt his problem could not be overcome by Jesus. He went back to that town and told people the great things God did for him. Someone might say, "Oh, yes, but you don't know how bad my situation is." The healed demonic could empathize with them and say, "Oh, yes, I do! But look, it's still possible."

**Application**

This is a story about twins. One was an extreme pessimist; the other was an extreme optimist. The problem became so bad that their parents had to take them to a psychiatrist. His solution was to put the pessimistic boy in a room full of toys, candy, ice cream and cake, and everything that makes a child happy. They were to put the optimistic boy in a room with only one thing, a large pile of horse manure. They put them in their rooms for an hour and checked on them. The parents went to the room of the pessimistic boy hoping to find him very happy, but he was doing nothing.

They said, "What's the matter, Johnny? Why don't you ride the horsey?"

He said, "I was afraid of falling off the horsey and breaking my leg."

"Why didn't you eat the ice cream?"

"Oh, I was afraid of getting a tummy ache!"

"Well, why didn't you do this…"

For everything, he had a negative response. It did not solve his problem. They went to the room of the optimistic boy. As they walked toward his room, they heard *splat, splish, swish, splash, splash, bang*. They opened the door very carefully, and they saw him bent over the manure pile. "What in the world are you doing, Jimmy?" they shouted.

"Mommy and Daddy, with all this horse manure around here, there's bound to be a pony somewhere!"

No matter how difficult life becomes, no matter how much the lives of others even smell and stink to us, love does not rejoice in unrighteousness but rejoices with the truth. By God's grace, we can rejoice in truth. We can give ourselves to those who are most deeply involved with sin, knowing their potential to love Christ more.

# LIFE MESSAGE 12

## *Love Bears All Things*

Viewing 37 movies in one week, believed to be the typical film fair showing around the country, a University of Utah psychologist and his research team saw 59 murders, 89 justifiable killings, 76 attempted murders, 11 massacres, 6 bombings, 3 assault rapes, 168 nude scenes, 19 acts of explicit intercourse, 3 acts of masturbation, 7 scenes of oral-genital activity, and a variety of seductive exhibitions. According to Victor B. Cline, that is 23 acts of violence and 15 episodes of sex per film. He believes movies and TV are headed for an era of unrelenting violence and exploitive sex. "By making violence appear glamorous and exciting and illicit sex normal and desirable, these media are setting the stage for a society based on aggression and irresponsibility," he said.

Other findings: two-thirds of the films took a fatalistic view of life and human destiny; 22 percent of the protagonists were killed or in some way destroyed. In 57 percent of the films, dishonesty was presented in a heroic light or justified; in 83 percent, criminal activity actually paid of—there were no negative consequences; in 43 percent, the heroes were lawbreakers or antisocial figures; in 60 percent, premarital sex was normal, acceptable, desirable; 70 percent of the heroes were to some degree sexually promiscuous.

In the TV ads for children, 20 salesmen per hour talk to them, half the time with sweets in hand. Robert Choate, chairman of the Council on Children, Media, and Merchandising, estimates that a moderate TV-watching child views more than 5,000 commercials for edibles every year. "Fifty percent of the advertising directed to children is on edibles. And the ethic is buy, spend, eat and consume," he said. The harm goes deeper than arguments over nutrition. The essential harm is the materialistic value it promote. "Our free enterprise system considers it is fair and proper for competition to advise kids to be materialistic and acquisitive, to keep up with the Joneses, govern health by artificial means, and to live in a world of fantasy," Mr. Choate says.

Mental depression increases. "If the 1950s were the age of anxiety, then the 1970s are the age of melancholy," says Dr. Gerald Klerman, professor of psychiatry at Harvard. Depression paralyzes the will, saps energy, and drives some to suicide. Doctors divide on cause; some blame stress, others say it is malfunction of the chemistry of the brain. Depression can hit several times during a lifetime and last up to six months at a time. Women sufferers outnumber men, two to one. It is twice as common among married people. Depression hits students especially hard and is a major cause of dropping out. Antidepressant drugs do not work with many people. Suicide rates with depressives is 30 times that of the general population. Very successful people are often subject to depression. Sexual and marital problems are the most common types of stress.

Divorces went to 80 percent between 1960 and 1971, according to the US Bureau of Census. Divorces averaged slightly more than 400,000 in the 1960–1962 period, but there were around 768,000 divorces in 1971. The study indicated that about 29 percent of the marriages of women now between 27 and 32 years of age will end in divorce. The average age for a woman's first marriage is now 20.8, compared to 20.3 in 1960.

Ralph Sorcom said, "The roots of responsibility run to the ends of the earth, and we can no more isolate our consciences from world issues than we can fence off our oyster beds from the tides of the ocean."

Yet that is exactly what most people are doing today, including those in the church. The church has a major problem because Christians tolerate too many things. They are too permissive. This destroys the spiritual fiber of the church and degenerates its witness. Christians can hide their eyes and pretend these problems do not exist. They can interpret 1 Corinthians 13:7's "Love bears all things" to mean that we just bear those things we can endure, we cover them over. We close our eyes to them; we do not pay attention to them. Therefore, Christians shirk their responsibilities and live self-centered, egocentric lives. However, Paul's statement "Love bears all things" really means we must bear the responsibility of all things. I'm embarrassed that although I checked twenty commentaries on this passage, I did not find one that spoke to this issue.

Therefore, we must approach this text with three basic steps: observation, interpretation, and application. Observation answers the question, what is its interpretation? Interpretation: what does it mean? Application: what does it mean to me?

## I. Observation of "Stegay" (Bears)

To observe, we ask six questions: who, what, when, where, why, and wherefore.

*A. Who?*

Who bears all things? Love. Love can also be a person. God is love. First Corinthians 13 is also a portrait of Jesus Christ Himself. The *who* could also be Christ. But because every Christian should be Christlike, the *who* is every believer.

*B. What?*

What here? All things. Love bears all things. It does not mean negative things only. Of course, love does bear somebody's stupidity, ignorance, or some irritating ways. But the text does not limit love to that. Love bears good things too.

*C. When?*

When does love bear all things? Well, if you look at the word *bear*, it is in the present tense. It is durative action. It is constantly going on without any thought of beginning or ending. The implication, of course, is love does not bear all things sometimes, and not other times.

Love is consistent.

*D. Where?*

Where? Love bears all things everywhere. If love bears all things at all times, then all places would be included. Love, for example, does not act one way inside the home and another way some other place outside the home.

*E. Whence?*

The word *whence* means "how." How does love bear all things? This verse does not say how. Why does not it tell us? Because Christ said, "You shall do and then you shall know." To obey is to know. In the doing is the knowing.

*F. Why?*

Why? Why does love bear all things? Because it is the very nature of love. It is unnatural for Christ, God, or the Christian to act in an impatient, unenduring way.

## II. Interpretation of "Stegay" (Bears)

We must go to the second step, interpretation. What is the interpretation of *stegay*? The word *stegay* is the Greek word for "bears."

*A. Cover*

There are two basic meanings of the word. The one meaning is "cover." It comes from the word for roof or covering. The idea is to protect people, to protect things. But this does not mean that love simply glosses over sin, for example. Covering a multitude of your brother's sins does not mean ignoring them, but rather ministering in love and humility to him so that he will repent. A person covers a multitude of sins by sparing his brother from successive sins, by spreading the link in the chain of sins. Love does not actually cover sin because the Bible says in Proverbs, "He who covers a transgression shall not prosper." We cannot apply this meaning of the word to love. Love does not cover bad habits but rather corrects them and exposes them.

*B. Endure*

The second meaning of the word *stegay* is endure. This means enduring something or somebody for a long period of time. This is passive. It leaves a person unfulfilled. Then, too, some things I enjoy so much that I don't have to endure them. Other things I do not endure at all because the Bible says to repent of certain things.

*C. Bear*

A third meaning of *stegay* is "bear," the idea of holding fast or containing the idea of bearing responsibility. This meaning rings the bell here, meaning to bear one's responsibility in all things. If we use the meaning of bearing responsibility in light of the six questions above, it fits all of them beautifully. It means controlling the selfish drives. It means being responsible in all things of life, whether at home, school, work, church, wherever we go.

## III. Application of "Stegay"

There are three priorities in life: our personal relationship to God, our relationship to our family, and our relationship to our life's work. The idea of love bearing all things must be applied to every one of these relationships.

Matthew Henry says, "Hearing all things in life means passing by and putting up with injuries without indulging in anger or cherishing revenge; will be patient upon provocation, ill-usage, curses, contumacies, slander, prison, exile, bonds, torments and even death itself. But all these things imply only the negative things we should bear. Let me add a few positive things, because all things means all positive as well as all negative things. Things like this: prayer, Bible reading, meditation, soul-winning, serving, punctuality, diligence, loyalty, faithfulness, discipline, faith, hope, love, food, clothing, shelter. Love bears all things."

*A. Our Relationship to God*

Love bears all things to God. Tithing money, for example. The Bible teaches at least 10 percent of our income should go to the Lord, without any excuses. Beyond that are offerings, love gifts, and grace giving, as the grace of God enables us to give liberally and hilariously.

What about our relationship to God in time? It has been well said that if a Christian would tithe his time, that would be 16.8 hours a week. If believers do that, every church would run beautifully and smoothly. How many Christians give 16.8 hours per week to serving God in the local church?

What about our talents? Christians can use a variety of talents for the Lord. Some of them never think of doing this. Yet this is something that love bears for the sake of Christ.

*B. Our Relationship to Family*

Do Christians "bear all things" with regard to their families? Do husbands love their wives as Christ loved the church? Do wives really submit to their husbands and husbands to their wives? Do children really honor their parents in the Lord? And do parents honor their children?

*C. Our Relationship to Work*

Bearing all things at work means doing your best at your job. Love does not just put in time. The believer should be really excited about his employer's success. He does not simply get his money the easiest way he can, with the least amount of effort.

## Application

A child was born into a Christian family, but it became apparent that he was suffering an incurable illness. As the little boy got older, the family had to decide whether or not they should put him into an institution. After discussion, the vote was unanimous; the child would remain at home. He was loved tenderly in spite of his mental and physical retardation. Finally, at the age of thirteen, he died. But all the family members turned to each other and said, "We have gained so much by giving so much. We have all learned how to be much more loving and kind, compassionate and understanding in treating other people as well as Tommy." Love bears all things. There are many weak people in the church. In the society, there are people who are spiritually dead. They are dead in trespasses and sin; they are bound for hell. Love bears a responsibility for all of them.

# LIFE MESSAGE 13

## *Love Believes All Things*

Some very interesting words have been said down through the centuries about faith. Our Lord Jesus Christ said, "Nothing shall be impossible to you" (Matt. 17:20). Augustine said, "Faith is to believe what we do not see, and the reward of this faith is to see what we believe."

Others have said, "The greatest victories are the victories of faith. It is not so much what we can do that counts, but what we can trust God to do." "Small faith may take you to heaven, but great faith may bring heaven to you." "We do not know one millionth of one part of one percent about anything. We do not know what water is; we do not know what light is; we do not know what electricity is; we do not know what gravity is. We do not know anything about magnetism. We have a lot of hypotheses, but that is all" (Thomas A. Edison).

But the Bible says, "Through faith we understand." Faith is exercised in relation to the world, to the church, and to the Christian.

## I. In Relation to the World

An article by Gerald H. Train, chairman of the Community Interfaith Emergency Service, Norristown, Pennsylvania, says in relation to our world:

> Our nation today stands on the brink of disaster. Its communities from the Atlantic to the Pacific, from Canada to Mexico, are being disrupted by the great drug epidemic which is breeding crimes of all types in order to feed the insatiable appetites of the addicts. Fear and hate stalk our villages and cities. Hunger and racial tensions weigh heavily in the ghettos and slums. Our elderly are living in dark forbidden times, instead of in the fulfillment of their golden years.
>
> Look with me for a moment in your imagination into a large transparent sphere where exist our communities. Here is what you'll see. The churches burdened with seemingly unsolvable inner problems of departing clergy, dropping membership roles, and drastically reduced giving, and lament entangled with the materialistic values of life. The social agencies running in ever tightening circles of frustration and desperation as the stream mounts swiftly to a flood of human misery, daily moving through their doors, seeking answers to problems that threaten their very existence. The community at large, splitting out of control, while being fragmented by corrupt politics, crimes of all degrees, growing drug problems, fear, hunger,

> sickness, racial tension and violent death itself. All these things comprise the world in which we live.

These insights arouse within me a great consternation. We have problems enough to solve among ourselves as Christians, let alone trying to solve the world's problems. Yet our responsibility is still there, because the Bible says, "Love believes all things" (1 Cor. 13:7).

How can a Christian "believe all things" in a world like this? Is it not unreasonable of God to expect us to believe all things in the face of a very troubled society, nation, and world? Do the words "Love believes all things" in relation to the world include every Christian? Yes, even though humanly it is an impossible task, God still expects you to fulfill it! It is unreasonable if you try to do it without faith. How can I solve the word's problems? By believing all things.

I used to say, "It's not great faith in a big God, but rather it's small faith in a big God. That's all it takes." But now I am beginning to see where we are responsible for great faith. Although we may start by having faith no bigger than a mustard seed, faith has to grow. As our Lord told the story, that tiny seed grew into a mighty tree. So we must face the ideal. Nothing is impossible unto him who believes all things, even in relation to a troubled world. Christians, therefore, by love must make some impact on the world.

### II. In Relation to the Church

In that great fourteenth chapter of John, verse 6, the Lord Jesus not only shows the way to heaven but also the way through our life in this world. He is the way through the problem of a fruitless, ignorant, weak, and foolish Christian life. He is the way to a more fruitful, powerful, glorious life for Him in this world.

One of the most beautiful experiences a person can ever have traveling in Norway is to sail through the majestic fjords. You sail past the sheer cliffs, with cascades of water splashing down, echoing their beautiful musical tones. You see high mountains and verdant green slopes. But when you approach the end of the fjord, as you get closer and closer, you are filled with fear because you think the ship is going to collide with the cliff. But at the last moment, in the nick of time, a whole new beautiful way opens up to another fjord. Life is like that, isn't it? The mountains are seemingly unmovable in our lives. Circumstances make us stop dead in our tracks. We either want to jump off the boat or stop the boat. We seemingly never reach the place where there is a way around it, under it, or through it. We never find out the way because we do not believe there is a way.

Faith finds a way always. The Lord Jesus Christ is that way. He never fails. The same Jesus Christ who said He is the way, the truth, and the life, also said, in Matthew 16:18, "Upon this rock I will build my church and the gates of hell will not prevail against it!" The iron gates of a fjord will not prevail against the assaults of the devil but will destroy his gates as it progresses forward.

David Livingstone said, "I'll go anywhere, as long as it's forward." That is the spirit of a real Christian. No wonder he went to Africa in all its darkness to bring light to that continent. That is the kind of spirit the church needs. Faith finds a way. Christ promised, "I will build my church." He did not start to build until after He went to heaven. On the day of Pentecost, He preached through Peter to that crowd of thousands. That was the way He began to build His church. Three thousand souls came to Christ and were added to the church; days after that, more came, five thousand, and it went on and on and on. Jesus Christ from the Father's right hand is still building His church. His only requirement is "all things are possible unto him who believes" for love believes all things. Our Lord Jesus Christ wants to build His church. Can we believe that in the face of all the problems in this world, we can be used by Him to build His church?

Jesus has chosen to build His church with foolish, weak, and inadequate building stones. According to 1 Peter 2:1, we are all living stones. He chooses to use us, but He does it by transforming us into building blocks in His kingdom. Unfortunately, because we persist in our folly, in our weakness, in our nothingness, we become stumbling blocks instead of building blocks.

On one occasion, John Wesley was walking down a country path with a friend. The friend shared how he had lost his faith over the years of Christian life and how despondent he was over the problem.

As he was talking they came to a cow. Wesley turned to his friend and said, "Brother, do you see that cow looking over the wall?"

"Yes."

"Why is that cow looking over the stone wall?" Wesley asked.

"I don't know. Tell me why."

"Because the cow can't see through it, that's why!"

Too often Christians are looking at the wall, trying to look through it. They cannot see anything. What a predicament. The answer is just a matter of looking over the wall, and faith does that sort of thing.

Faith is so great that it causes those who are really spiritual in the congregation not to leave when a brother transgresses or stumbles. The ones who are spiritual are bolstered by faith to pick up and restore those who stumble. The church should be a place of security like that. When we stumble, we should be surrounded by a cloud of dear, loving Christians who, in meekness and gentleness, pick up and restore us. That is what faith does as it builds the church.

Faith enables a congregation of people really to believe that they can reproduce spiritually by going out and winning souls. A founding pastor says, "We at Christ Church of Valley Forge have just passed our fourth anniversary. We are also just about filling a 275-seat auditorium. But as long as we keep seeing empty seats, no matter how big the building, we are seeing a stone wall. In our churches, all believers must look above the wall and so do their part in leaping over it, to bring in others to fill the empty chairs."

You know the story Jesus told about the wedding feast. The king himself made invitations for all the neighbors to come to a lovely wedding feast, but only a few came. What did he tell his servants? He told them to go into the highways and byways and hedges to seek people, to bring in the poor, the blind, the maimed, the weak, and the sick. Many people are maimed, blind, and sick spiritually. They have lost their hope. Their hearts are sick and burdened with heavy cares. Christians must reach out to them. Can love motivate you to go out to your neighbors and bring them the feast of a message of hope in Christ? Faith believes and makes you believe you can do that.

### III. In Relation to the Christian

There is another realm of love that believes all things, that is in relation to the Christian: 1) the Christian in relation to another Christian, and 2) the Christian in relation to himself. Regarding the first aspect, the Christian should unsuspiciously believe all that is not palpably false, all that he can with a good conscience believe to the credit of another (James 32:17). On the surface, this appears as though love is soft and credulous, easily taken in by any doer of evil. But the truth is that one must live either in a state of trust or in a state of suspicion toward his fellows and himself. There really is not a middle ground. Either we go through life cynically suspecting everybody and turning out to be wrong most of the time, or basically we go through life believing in the good of others and turning out to be wrong part of the time.

We can take our choice, but from a purely practical standpoint, our happiness is at stake in the way we go. If we are basically cynical, we do not want to be wrong about anything, for to be wrong is to prove the folly of our cynicism. And if we are right, which on occasion we will most certainly be, what satisfaction can we possible get out of that?

Really, distrusting people does not do us any good. There is a story about a woman who used to say complacently, "I'm very frank. I always believe in being honest and open." She was, in fact, frank to the point of untenderness. If there was a weakness in the character of any of her friends, she pointed it out with the most devastating bluntness. She was fond of telling others what she thought they ought to do. Her frankness was a camouflage for being mean. When it came to those not equally blunt, she always said, "I wouldn't trust her as far as I could see her, too mealymouthed." We tend to put our trust in our own strong points rather than in the Lord. As a result, we distrust everyone whose strength lies in something else.

You may be an introvert and therefore say, "But there are certain people who make me feel uncomfortable." Then look at the words of A. B. Simpson: "You will never learn faith in comfortable surroundings." Some of the very people we do not believe in, and consequently avoid, are the very ones whom God will reveal to you at the judgment seat as the very "instruments" that He chose to shape you more into His own image. Do not pass up such an opportunity of growth.

The truth is that to love men in the sense in which Paul is using the term is to believe in the best in them and often to believe in the best to help it come into being. Many a young man has done fine things with his life because others believed he would and he knew it. Many a fine girl has accomplished fine things with her life that she never would have accomplished except that there were those who loved her and believed she would.

Of course, it works the other way around also. To hold someone in contempt is to run the risk of making that person worthy of our contempt. More than one husband living with a suspicious wife, and more than one wife living with a suspicious husband, has seriously raised the question, "Why not? I am believed to be guilty anyway, and I cannot possibly prove that I am not." Many a person has rationalized and justified behavior of an evil sort in advance of performance on the ground that he might just as well be guilty as to be accused and believed by others to be so.

The other side of the coin is the skepticism with which we view our own weaknesses. It is possible to be entirely immobilized because we are so sure of our failure. Or to say of someone else, "He won't stick to it, of course, he has never been able to see anything through." In short, it's very difficult for us to believe either that we will come crashing down some day in one of our strong areas or that we can succeed in the weak ones. Our trust is in ourselves, not in Christ at all.

Perhaps it's a good thing that we all fail once in a while, in the very area where we've been most successful, and that we see unexpected triumph in places of defeat. Human nature is unpredictable, we say at such times, but the truth is that the way God works is unpredictable and He does not intend for us to be too sure of anything but Himself…it is too dangerous for us.

Handel had to face failure in his musical career, as well as financial bankruptcy. He was even threatened with prison. He faced such serious sickness that his right side became paralyzed. In that condition, at the point of despair, God finally came to him. As a result, he produced *Messiah* with its great "Hallelujah Chorus."

Failure may teach us not to be too sure of our strengths, especially, or to be too unbelieving about our weaknesses. It can bring us to that point where only God Himself will bolster us up, carry us on, and teach us the lesson that He is in everything.

But why stop at this? Why not believe all things just like Eileen Guder, who lost her husband shortly after the roof of their house caved in one night during a storm. Eileen Guder's son died at an early age. Her financial future crashed before her. She said, "Believing all things about life in a baseless optimism helps me not at all. Being naive like that helps me not one single bit in my agonies of life." But she added, "Believing everything because God is in it, that strengthens me!"

Such an attitude is similar to that of another exceptional individual who believed all things even when his only son was killed. When Sir Harvey Lauder's only son was killed in World War I, he said to a friend, "When a man comes to a thing like this, there are just three ways out of it. There is drink, there is despair, and there is God. By His grace, the last one is for me."

Let us move on to the Christian in relation to himself. Here is where the real problem lies. After many years in education, business, and especially in the ministry, I am convinced that the average Christian has a difficult and almost impossible time believing all things about himself, just as he has a great difficulty loving himself. Satan does such a good job of deceiving the Christian that he actually feels it is a sin to have confidence, or belief, even in his new self in Christ. Many Christians do not know how to believe for their own benefit. I want to share with you an acrostic on the word *belief* that has helped tens of thousands of people both in the secular and religious world.

We will assume that we are sharing this little device with a person whose faith is either shattered or is not at all developed. We shall start at zero. The key question is, how does one grow in belief from zero? Whether it is to believe in Christ Himself, or in one's God-given ability and talents by which to serve Him, how does one grow in belief?

To answer this question, we shall take the word belief and form an acrostic, so that

*B* stands for boldness
*E* stands for excellence
*L* stands for liability
*I* stands for insistence
*E* stands for endurance
*F* stands for faith

Obviously the purpose of this acrostic is simple memorization by the reader, so he can carry it with him wherever he goes. Now let us go into more detail.

*B* stands for boldness. Here is the starting point. If one ever intends to believe in anything, he must eventually be bold enough to make that leap of faith! This is necessary whether it is to believe in the Lord Jesus Christ as one's Savior and God because of His purchasing heaven as a gift by His death on the cross, or whether it is to believe in accomplishing some seemingly difficult or impossible work. This boldness should be one of the first things that people see in a Christian. In Acts

4:13, Luke says, "Now when they saw the boldness of Peter and John, and perceived that they were unlearned and ignorant men, they marveled; and they took knowledge of them, that they had been with Jesus" (King James Version).

The early Christians were "dumb enough to be bold in their belief." They did not complicate it like we do, but rather they were childlike in their faith. Being uneducated was not an obstacle. Believing in Jesus was all they needed. As a result, people marveled that they had been with Jesus! So can it be for you and me.

We lack boldness because we have our eyes too much upon the obstacles of our belief. Think on this anonymous poem:

Doubt sees the obstacles,
Faith sees the way,
Doubt sees the darkest night,
Faith sees the day!
Doubt dreads to take a step,
Faith soars on high,
Doubt questions, "Who believes?"
Faith answers, "I!"

Do you see the possibility of budging your inertia of doubt? Believe and it will grow. One of the names for a Christian is "believer." Yet it is so unfortunate that so many who have been born again are for the most part mediocre in faith. We say, on the one hand, that we believe in the God of miracles. Yet, on the other hand, our lives deny that belief. Faith without works is dead.

Too often we are communicating to the world that our God is the God of mediocrity, not the God of miracles. We say Amen to the words "Love believes all things," but we do not make changes regarding our doubts.

Some aspirants who desired to scale Mount Everest were examined by a psychologist at Nepal before they began their climb. They were asked, "Will you get to the top?" One said, "I certainly hope so." Another said, "I'll try." Another, "I'll do my best." Only Jim Whitaker replied, "Yes, I will." And only Jim made it. He was the first American to reach the summit of Everest. "Mountain climbing brings out the best in a person," said Whitaker. "It forces him to try something normally beyond his reach." Browning said, "A man's reach should exceed his grasp, or what's heaven for?"

Is it not time that Christians, by faith in God, claim their heritage in boldness and move forward from spinning wheels in the mudhole of mediocrity to springing zeal in the mountain of miracles.

*E* stands for excellence. There is no reason to move out of mediocrity unless we go all the way to excellence, for that should be the believer's only standard. The Lord Jesus Christ commanded, "Therefore you are to be perfect, as your heavenly Father is perfect" (Matt. 5:48). Yes, He said these words in the Sermon on the Mount to Jews who were about to enter the Kingdom of God, but his words contain a principle that can be applied to all of us. That is why the Apostle Paul also commanded, "Let us therefore, as many as are perfect, have this attitude; and if in anything you have a different attitude, God will reveal that also to you: However, let us keep living by that same standard to which we have attained. Brethren, join in following my example, and observe those who walk according to the pattern you have in us" (Phil. 3:15–17).

An anonymous individual put it this way: "There are peaks of holiness and Christian virtue which ever beckon and challenge us in our upward path. Let us not be content to hang on to a cliff halfway up. Let us get to the top."

Solomon in the inspired writings of Ecclesiastics put it another way: "Whatever your hand finds to do, verily, do it with all your might."

Where is the Christian who will do his best in his work and strive for excellence in all that he does? Where is the person who should be a Christian but is not because of the bad advertisements of Christianity he has seen in other Christians? Is it not time for all of us to ignore the obstacles and progress toward excellence, which comes through our belief in the Lord Jesus Christ? Do we not all realize that we are responsible to be perfect, whether Christian or non-Christian? If not, we are left to our hell in hell as well as in our hell on earth! It is true that in ourselves and of ourselves, we are inadequate. But we can be made perfect as well as excellent through Christ. That is why God reveals though the Apostle Paul. "Just as He chose us in Him before the foundation of the world, that we should be holy and blameless before Him" (Eph. 1:4). This holiness and blamelessness is nothing less than God's standard of perfection for man.

Well, then, how does one get it? Look at Ephesians 1:7. "In Him (Christ) we have redemption through His blood, the forgiveness of our trespasses, according to the riches of His grace." That is how. Look at it this way. When you first believe in Christ, you accept the fact that Christ Jesus the Lord sacrificed His perfect life on the cross for your rather imperfect (sinful) life. In response to your faith, God graciously forgives you from all your sins and positions you in Christ. Thus, in Christ, you are positionally perfect. He also promises you that you will be perfect in heaven forever. In the meanwhile, between the time you first really believe in Christ and the time you go to heaven, you are to work at matching your practice with your position. That is to say, that one day at a time you are to surrender your thoughts, words, actions, to the standard of perfection that is in

Christ. Yes, you will stumble, but you will get up and continue. Living in such a style, your trend is upward and certainly higher than any other lifestyle you would have otherwise.

If you do not know how to overcome your past at this point, listen to the words of the Apostle Paul: "Not that I have already obtained it, or have already became perfect, but I press an in order that I may lay hold of that for which also I was laid hold of by Christ Jesus. Brethren, I do not regard myself as having laid hold of it yet; but one thing I do: forgetting what lies behind and reaching forward to what lies ahead, I *press* on toward the goal for the prize of the upward call of God in Christ Jesus." (Phil. 3:12–14).

Every believer can rise above the soft and mediocre environment of our materialistic age and press on toward God's true mark of excellence!

*L* stands for liability. Just what do we mean by the liability of faith? Webster defines *liability* as "the state of being exposed to danger." Such a definition is pertinent to our point here because living by faith certainly does expose us to danger. Thus, a great caution from God's word, "Therefore let him who thinks he stands take heed lest he fall" (1 Cor. 10:12).

Instinctively, we are all afraid. We are afraid to move ahead because we do not know what is there, and is our fear well founded? Is it not true that most things we fear never happen? A young businessman addressing a sales convention somehow came up with the figure of 90 percent, but certainly it makes the point that we fear too much. On this point, I highly recommend Tim LaHaye's book *Spirit-Controlled Temperament*, which has an excellent chapter on fear, showing the great costs of fear.

It is important, however, to stress what we should really fear.

Martin Luther said, "My greatest enemy is not the people who try to assassinate me, not the demons, nor even the devil himself, but rather my greatest enemy is my own deceitful heart." Our greatest liability is our own deceitful hearts. No wonder the prophet Jeremiah said, "The heart is deceitful above all else and is desperately sick; who can understand it?" (Jer. 17:9).

I stand for insistence. It is not intelligence, but rather insistence. I do not minimize the necessity of intelligence, but neither do I maximize it. This priority fits together in 1 Corinthians 1:26–29: "For consider your call, brethren, that there were not many wise according to the flesh, not many mighty, not many noble; but Gad has chosen the foolish things of the world to shame the wise, and God has chosen the weak things of the world to shame the things which are strong, and the basest things of the world and the despised, God has chosen, the things that are not, that He might nullify the things that are, that no man should boast before God."

The question could well be raised, how does God shame the wise and mighty by choosing the foolish and the weak? There are two ways:

1. By His choice of man, which is based upon His unconditional love and not the ability of man.
2. By His synergizing power by which He transforms the foolish into wise and the weak into might. There is a dynamic potential in this for every believer.

Although God chose the foolish and weak, He does not intend us to stay that way! On the contrary, he desires to transform us by His power from foolishness into wisdom, from weakness into might. When people who know you see your changed life, they will be amazed, confounded, and shamed by what they see, realizing that only God Himself could have changed you like that. If this is not true of all of us, it is because we lack insistence. There is the quality of faith that Christ had in mind when He commanded, "Have faith in God. Truly I say to you, whoever says to this mountain, 'Be taken up and cast into the sea,' and does not doubt in his heart, but believes that what he says is going to happen; it shall be granted him. Therefore, I say to you, all filings for which you pray and ask, believe that you have received them, and they shall be granted you." (Mark 11:22–24).

True belief in Christ is an insisting belief that will not doubt. Do you pray like that? Do you move toward your goals like that? Do you work like that? Unfortunately, most Christians pray with the pestilence of doubt, not the insistence of belief.

To be sure, your faith is according to God's will. Begin with God's Word and insist by faith that God be true to His promises, that He perform miracles in your life, things like changing your behavior, your witnessing, your godly presence as salt of the earth and light of the world. You are on safe ground, believing that these things are God's will because the Bible says so. Second, obey the above scripture by really learning how to pray. Notice that little clause in verse 24, "Pray and ask." It reminds us of James 5:16–17, describing the praying of Elijah: "The effectual prayer of a righteous man availeth much. Elijah was a man subject to passions as we are, and he prayed earnestly" (King James Version). This is the key to faith.

In the words of George Muller, "The great point is never give up until the answer comes. The great fault of the children of God is, they do not continue in prayer; they do not persevere. If they desire anything for God's glory, they should pray until they get it!"

That is the only way you can know what God's will is in the circumstances of life outside the pages of the Bible. But beware of even the subtle doubts once you know. Dr. Samuel Zwemer said, "Faith is the outstretched hand of the soul, taking what Christ offers. Faith is what made the little girl take an umbrella to the prayer meeting called especially to pray for rain! The grown-ups wore sun glasses."

Only by earnest, fervent belief and prayer will you move mountains and accomplish great things for God.

*E* stands for endurance. Our Lord said, "But the one who endures to the end, it is he who shall be saved" (Matt. 24:13). This passage has dispensational overtones that I accept, but I also accept the principle that is inherent in it for all of us. Taking the verse at face value, we must apply it to ourselves in solemn self-examination. What it simply means in principle is that unless we endure our belief in Christ, we will not be saved by Christ in this life or in the next.

At the end of His Sermon on the Mount, our Lord further clarified this point: "Not everyone who says to me on that day (Judgment Day), 'Lord, Lord,' will enter the Kingdom of Heaven; but he who does the will of My Father, which is in Heaven." (Matt. 7:21). He exposes the true nature of faith, which is not just the ability to say words like *Lord*, but also the ability to do the will of the Father even to the Day of Judgment. This is what John Calvin meant by the doctrine of perseverance of the saints. The true believer cannot lose his salvation, for he is eternally secure (Phil. 1:6), but the true believer also endures to the end by shaping his behavior according to the Father's will. It is true that a believer cannot lose his salvation, but it is also true that while many people profess to be believers, that does not mean that they are. We have no right to give assurance of salvation to anyone, unless he keeps enduring to do the Father's will.

What about the carnal Christians? There are such Christians, but I do not believe that the popular notion of the carnal Christian is what Paul meant in 1 Corinthians 3:1–3. The popular notion of a carnal Christian portrays him as a backsliding idler and an apathetic believer.

What a contrast this is to the carnal Christian portrayed in 1 Corinthians 3:1–3. There he is presented as progressive, active, and energetic in the flesh instead of in the spirit. Those carnal Christians at Corinth were playing favorites between the great Christian leaders of their day. Therefore, they caused divisions. That is why Paul called them carnal. We have no right to give assurance of salvation to a backslidden, idle, and/or apathetic person who professes to be a believer, as though we viewed him to be a "carnal" Christian. That is not a carnal Christian.

There is a great danger in robbing some believer of his assurance, but there is the greater danger in robbing some believer of his assurance to a person. Love does not give a person false assurance. Even though love believes all things, love is not so naive and presumptuous as to tell a person he is going to heaven, when in reality he is going to hell.

If a Christian stumbles into sin, 1) it is the responsibility of the spiritual believer to restore him (Gal. 6:1); 2) it is the responsibility of the sinning believer to get up and go on, even if he falls seven times (Prov. 24:16); 3) it is the responsibility of God to come to his aid (Ps. 37:23–24; Jude 24); and 4)it is the responsibility of angels to minister to him (Heb. 1:14). With such a fourfold force keeping the real believer on the straight and narrow path, I seriously question any believer who stays off the path too long.

What about discouragements? Meditate on the words of George Muller: "I have not met with many discouragements; but at all times my confidence has been in God. On the word of Jehovah's promise my soul rests! Oh, it is good to trust in Him; His word never returns void! 'He gives power to the faint and to them that have no might, He increases strength' (Isa. 40:29)."

True, George Muller was an exceptional man of faith, but listen to his exhortations. "Does the Lord love you less than lie loves us? Does He not love all His children with no less love than that with which He loves His only begotten son, according to John 17:20–23? Are we better than you?"

Why did I go to such lengths about endurance? Because in these last days, there appear to be many people professing Christ, but they do not possess any kind of quality of enduring Christ. The slightest demands of discipleship cause them to avoid the local church. The slightest touch of persecution triggers them into compromise. The slightest hint that their sinful lives must be changed into holy lives makes them retaliate. "I thought salvation was through faith and not works?" they say. Such people, no matter what they say, are not really believers.

What a contrast such professors are to the possessor Paul, who declared, "Thou, therefore, endure such hardness, as a good soldier of Jesus Christ. Therefore, I endure all things for the elect's sake, that they may obtain the salvation which is in Christ Jesus with eternal glory" (2 Tim. 2:3, 10, KJV). The kind of love that believes all things, also believes that endurance must be a supreme characteristic for the believer.

*F* stands for fight. The last step in the development of one's belief is *fight*. The Christian, having been justified through faith, has peace with God. But the Christian life is also a fight. The Bible declares, "Finally be strong in the Lord, and in the strength of His might. Put on the full armor of God, that you may be able to stand firm against the schemes of the devil. For our struggle is not against flesh and blood, but against the rulers, against the powers, against the world forces of darkness, against the spiritual forces of wickedness in the heavenly places. Therefore, take up the full armor of God, that you may be able to resist in the evil day, and having done everything to stand firm" (Eph. 6:10–13).

You do not have to be a Christian long before you fight against the above realities. As a matter of fact, the new believer or the revived believer who grows enthusiastically in his faith will quickly face opposition by Satan. Consequently, Paul appropriately exhorts us to take up "the shield of faith with which you will be able to extinguish all the flaming missiles of the evil one" (Eph. 6:16). Furthermore, to the degree that the believer grows in faith, to that degree, he will have to fight for every inch of ground he attains. Nor does such a fight cease, for at the end of his life, Paul said, "I have fought the good fight; I have finished the good fight of faith."

## Application

*Belief*! *B* stands for boldness; *E* for excellence; *L* for liability; *I* for insistence; *E* for endurance; *F* for fight—*B-E-L-I-E-F.* This is important because love believes all things. Do you believe like that? Let me give you a final secret about acquiring such belief.

Centuries ago, in the land of Greece, a young man walked up to Socrates, the great philosopher, and asked, "Socrates, will you share with me the secret of wisdom?"

Socrates, in reply, said, "Young man, do you realize that for which you are asking?"

The young man said, "Yes."

Then Socrates stood up, began to walk toward the lake, and said, "Follow me."

The young man did. The next thing he knew, he and Socrates were walking deeper and deeper into the water until they were shoulder deep.

Then Socrates said, "Turn around and face away from me." As soon as the young man did that, suddenly Socrates with his 210-pound body, swept out of the water and over the lad. Squeezing a death grip on him, Socrates held him under the water until he saw bubbles floating to the surface. Then he let the young man go.

As he came struggling and choking to the surface, he cried out, "What were you trying to do to me?"

Then came Socrates' secret for wisdom. He said, "Young man, when you seek for wisdom like you sought for air, you shall find it. That is the secret for wisdom!"

Likewise, believer, when you seek for belief like that young man sought for air, you, too, shall find it. That is also the secret for developing belief.

# LIFE MESSAGE 14

## *Love Hopes All Things*

Sir Winston Churchill stated, "I am an old man. I have lived a long time. I have never seen days like these. I am tired of it all. I see no hope for the future. Our problems are beyond us." Those are the words of one of the great men of our century, a man who well understood the condition of our world.

Words like *hope*, *love*, and *faith* are very difficult to understand, even by the greatest of men, because we have drained them of their content. They have become empty words because of world wars and because of many personal disappointments. It is hard to recover their meaning, to once again be inspired by their reality.

Winston Churchill's pessimism is a common attitude today held by more than a few people. Why? Because what the world calls hope is not true hope. What many Christians call hope is not true hope. True hope can be found only in the Lord Jesus Christ. It is not something based on anything other than Christ. Whatever we want to console ourselves with, we can be sure it will not stand the test of trials in our time.

Apart from Christ, we finally come to the place reflected in the words of Churchill.

Hopelessness is a real problem in our time. But it has always been that way. In every age, there have been trials that test faith and hope. Where does that lead us? What can we say in answer to the question, so why hope about anything, anytime? How many times have you been disappointed, when you had hope? We raise the question many times, if we are honest. How well are we grafted into Christ, whereby you live everyday believing and hoping all things? If that is not your normal Christian experience, then 1 Corinthians 13:7 is a message for you.

## Love Is Optimistic

"Love bears all things. Love believes all things. Love hopes all things."

Why? How can we really say that? How can we honestly, courageously, boldly, confidently, and even dogmatically say there is hope, hope for me, my family, and everybody with whom I share this wonderful truth?

Notice first of all that we are to hope in the meaning of life itself.

Secondly, there is hope in the mode of life that God has ordained through Christ. Lastly, there is hope in the motive of life.

## I. Hope in the Meaning of Life

Let us first consider hope in the meaning of life. The text emphasizes that love hopes all things. In other words, love is invincibly optimistic, for even when it suffers defeat, it will not quit, lest it fall short of hoping all things. Love never knows when it has lost a battle, so it keeps on hoping.

Such an attitude reminds me of a ten-year-old boy who was *very* optimistic about his baseball ability. His father was curious to find out just how optimistic he was, so one day he decided to play ball with him. He teased him, saying, "I'm going to strike you out the first time you're up to bat."

His son replied, "Oh no you're not! I'm a good batter!"

The father pitched the ball over the plate.

The boy swung and missed.

The father shouted, "That's strike one!" Again the father threw the ball over the plate.

This time the boy swung harder, and missed again.

And the father shouted, "That's strike two!" He threw the ball for the third time *over* the plate.

This time the son gave it all he had as he swung with all his might, but again he missed.

He heard his father shout, "That's strike three!" as he fell to the ground, having swung his bat so hard.

Then came the crucial moment. His father, as he stood there looking at his son on the ground, asked himself, *Was I too hard on the boy? Did I hurt his spirit?*

Within moments, the boy got right back up, dusted himself off, and said, "Boy, am I a good pitcher! Come on, Dad, you're up to bat!" That is being invincibly optimistic.

### *A. Not Because the World Is a Nice Place to Live In*

But we cannot think for a moment that Christian optimism is a Pollyanna buoyancy of good spirits. Christians do not have hope because the world is a nice place to live in. Christians do not have optimism because society is basically good. Nor do Christians have hope because they reinforce themselves with positive thinking, or with all sorts of pills and drugs.

*B. But Because There Is a Point to Living*

On the contrary, the Christian keeps on hoping on the basis of the conviction that because God is God, all fine ideals will someday become reality. For the Christian, there is hope because there is a point to living, and that point is the assurance that God lives and works in men and in the world. The Christian optimistically looks forward to that which God is doing in history. With absolutely optimistic enthusiasm, the Christian hopes in God, who has a purpose for all things, even though the Christian doesn't always understand the times of men and things. That is why Paul wrote in Romans 8:28, "And we know that God causes all things to work together for good to those who love God, to those who are called according to His purpose."

The Christian does not live in a world of fantasy, but rather he is convinced that regardless of what may go wrong, regardless of what sufferings he must go through, one day it will all be worth it.

> For I consider that the sufferings of the present tune are not worthy to be compared with the glory that is to be revealed to us. For the anxious longing of the creation waits eagerly for the revealing of the sons of God. For the creation was subjected to futility, not of its own will, but because of Him who subjected it, in hope that the creation itself also will be set free from its slavery to corruption into the freedom of the glory of the children of God. For we know that the whole creation groans and suffers the pain of childbirth together until now. And not only this, but also we ourselves, having the first fruits of the Spirit, even we ourselves groan

> within ourselves waiting eagerly for adoption as sons, the redemption of our body. For in hope we have been saved, but hope that is seen is not hope; for wiry does one false hope for what he sees? But if we hope for what we do not see, with perseverance we wait eagerly for it.
>
> (Rom. 8:18–25)

Some people disdain such hope by saying that Christians are dreamers. But I cannot imagine a more realistic outlook on life than that expressed above. The Apostle Paul encourages Christians to be constant in doing good without losing heart, not because things might work out well in this life necessarily, but because nothing they did would ever be lost or wasted in the eternal purpose of God. As Eileen Guder says it, "There would be a final solution, and all patient waiting would be rewarded, in God's time." That is why Dorothy L. Sayers is correct in observing, in her preface to *Man Born to Be King*, that no Christian tragedy is possible! Tragedy implies no hope, inevitable, unalterable doom. But that is not the message of the Bible. That is not the meaning of life.

> For in Him all things were created, both in heaven and on earth, visible and invisible, whether thrones or dominions or rulers or authorities, all things have been created through Him and for Him. And He is before all things, and in Him all things hold together. He is also the Head of the body, the church; and He is the beginning, the firstborn from the dead; so that He Himself might come to have first place in everything. For it was through the Father's

> good pleasure for all the fullness to dwell in Him, and through Him to reconcile all things to Himself, having made pence through the blood of His cross; through Him, I say, whether things ill earth or things in Heaven.
>
> (Col. 1:16–20)

## II. Hope in the Mode of Life

Let us move on to the Christian's hope in the mode of life. The question logically arises, what should be the lifestyle, or the mode of the Christian's life? The answer is rest.

### *A. Rest in the Hope That Is God*

If the reason to hope is that there is a point to life guaranteed by God, then we can relax or rest in the realization that our hope, above all things, is God himself. "Who through Him (Christ) are believers ill God, who raised Him (Christ) from the dead and gave him (Christ) glory, so that your faith and hope are ill God" (1 Pet. 1:21).

### *B. Rest in the Hope That Is Good*

Such a hope is good and genuine because it comes from God himself. It is not one of the vain hopes of the world that comes to us from political speeches, unloyal friends, or overly positive promises of prosperity. We can rest in the hope that is good because God gave it to us: "Now may our Lord Jesus Christ Himself and God our Father, who has loved us and given us eternal comfort and good hope by grace, com fort and strengthen your hearts in every good work and word" (2 Thess. 2:16–17).

The "rest" of the Christian does not make him lazy or passive, but rather calm and restful in attitude. As a matter of fact, the restful hope of the Christian strengthens him to work harder in the will of God because energy he would spend in worry and frustration is channeled into his life's work.

How different this attitude is in contrast to that of Jean Paul Sartre, as expressed in quotation from him, which I once memorized but have since forgotten the source from which it came. Nevertheless, expressing a widely prevalent and increasingly popular belief among intellectuals—negative existentialism—Jean Paul Sartre once said, "Man can count on no one but himself. He is alone, abandoned on earth in the midst of infinite responsibilities, without hope, with no other aim than the one he sets for himself, with no other destiny than the one he forges for himself on this earth." How hopeless and purposeless life is for those who embrace this negative belief. How worthy and satisfying life is for those who live for Christ and others.

### *C. Rest in the Hope That Is Growing*

It is a growing hope because it is a living hope. It is a growing hope because it begins with a rebirth, with being born again, with spiritual regeneration of God's life into ours. It is a growing hope because we grow into it daily. But do not forget, growth requires growing pains. "Blessed be God and the Father of our Lord Jesus Christ, who according to His great mercy has caused us to be born again to a living hope through the resurrection of Jesus Christ from the dead." (1 Pet. 1:3).

A long time ago, Robert Bruce, the king of Scotland, was forced to hide from his enemies. He found refuge in a cave deep in the forest. He was downhearted and discouraged. He had tried to save Scotland from her enemies, but he had lost every battle. His soldiers had been killed, wounded, and forced to hide. "It is of no use to fight anymore," he said. "Our enemies are too strong for us." Just then, he saw a spider weaving its web. She was trying to spin the web between two rocks. She had fastened one end of her thread to a rock and was trying to swing herself across but each time failed to reach the other side.

Bruce sat watching her for a long time. He wondered how long she would keep on trying. The spider tried and failed seven times. "You are a brave and patient spider," thought the king. "If you try once more and succeed I, too, will fight again." She did. "Thanks for the lesson you have taught me, little spider," said Bruce. "I will try once more to free Scotland from her enemies."

So King Robert Bruce went forth once again at the head of his army. He and his men fought as they had never fought before. Bruce won the battle, and his country was freed.

*D. Rest in the Hope That Is Groovy*

Really, I cannot think of a better word to describe 1 John 3:3. "And everyone who has this hope in him purifies himself, just as He is pure." The word *purifies* can certainly mean to groove our ways into God's ways. Is not the whole method of God in our lives to groove our lifestyle into His? The hope that God gives us is groovy.

*E. Rest in the Hope That Is Girded*

Peter tells us to be "sober and hope to the end" (1 Pet. 1:13). Gird your minds for action. The cold, dark world is no match for the Christian who is girded by hope.

The Irish essayist and lecturer George Bernard Shaw sums up the hopelessness of his own barren life and philosophy in the epigram: "There are two tragedies in life. One is not to get your heart's desire. The other is to get it." But Shaw is talking about the desire of the heart of the natural man, who knows not God nor Christ, and whose life is only death. He speaks truly when he says that, when such a man has gotten his heart's desire, he finds in it only disappointment, emptiness, and dissatisfaction. That is why so many today, both old and young people, having won their heart's desire, commit suicide.

*F. Rest in the Hope That Is Gratifying*

Paul tells us in Titus 2:13, "Looking for that blessed hope and appearing of the glory of our great God and Savior." This blessed hope is gratifying because it floods our subconscious through our eyes of hope. This is significant because psychologists tell us if we meditate on anything three different times with real concentration and earnestness, our subconscious receives the effect of such meditation equally as it would the actual event itself. That is to say our subconscious does not know the difference between that which is meditated on in such a threefold manner and that which actually has happened. Both affect the subconscious in the same way. Is this not hope that is gratifying? So hope on, my friend, hope on!

*G. Rest in the Hope That Is Glorious*

In the same verse we see that our hope is also glorious, for it shall be consummated in the literal appearing of our great God and Savior, Jesus Christ. All history is moving toward a consummation point, so history is really His story.

If love proves wrong, if believing in the best, the worst is nevertheless done, and if the offense proves to be a fact that can no longer be overlooked or condoned, love still does not give up. Love bears all things, it believes all things, and when proved to be wrong, then it resorts to hoping all things, ever allowing for the possibility that the penitent will do better. Hope sees the bright side of things; it doesn't despair.

It is certainly remarkable that both faith and hope are here predicated of love. This implies that hope and faith arise from love. When we love somebody, we trust him fully, we expect nothing but good things in return from him even though appearance be against him.

Love as far as it can with any reason will hope for the best and will stretch its faith beyond appearance for the support of a kind opinion; it will go into a bad one only with the utmost reluctance and force against it as much as it fairly and honestly can. And when, in spite of inclination, it cannot believe well, it will hope well and continue to hope as long as there is any ground for it. With such a God-given, good, growing, groovy, girded, gratifying, and glorious hope, how can we not hope?

### III. Hope in the Motive of Love

True Christian love produces hope in the motive of life. Why is it of all of the wonderful traits of love in 1 Corinthians 13, faith, hope, and love alone abide and yet the greatest of these is love?

Because it is only love that fully motivates us to do our best in life for God and man and ourselves. In 2 Corinthians 5:11, we see that the fear of God is a great motive for life. Even the Apostle Paul needed this type of motivation. When our love for God ceases to motivate us to do God's will, then we would better fear, for "the fear of God is the beginning of wisdom" (Prov. 9:10). Paul stresses fear as a proper motive for our lives.

But look also at 2 Corinthians 5:14: "For the love of Christ controls us." The word *controls* is a powerful word. It certainly means to motivate, but it also means to constrain, to dominate, to consume. To be sure, any Christian who is under such an influence as this will be filled with hope.

The greatest motive in life is the love of Christ. Let's hope in this motive. Hope in the love of Christ and you will have a life that hopes all things. It is an unfailing law. Try it and see.

Love hopes all things, and "all things" includes anything, no matter how despairing. Just take note of some of the following inspirational gems:

Harriet Beecher Stowe once said, "When you get into a tight place and everything goes against you until it seems you cannot hold on a minute longer, never give up then, for it is just the place and time when the tide will turn."

Lord Byron in "The Bride of Abydos" said of hope, "Be thou the rainbow to the storms of life, the evening beam that smiles the clouds away and tints tomorrow with prophetic ray."

Le Rochefould said, "We promise according to our hopes and perform according to our fears."

Peter describes the Christian's inheritance as a "living hope" (1 Pet. 1:3). That is in striking contrast to the hope of the world, for the worldly hopes men set their hearts upon fail them.

California for many years had a higher percentage of suicide than any other state. At first that seems strange when one reflects upon its beautiful scenery, its blue skies, and bright sunlight. Life, one would think, ought to be easier there than anywhere else. Why then so many suicides? The reason ascribed is that many have gone to California with what has been a last hope, either as to their health or their personal fortune, and when this hope failed them, life had nothing left for them. But the believer according to Peter has been begotten, born into a living hope.

## Application

When Abraham Lincoln was a young man, he ran for the legislature in Illinois and was overwhelmingly defeated. He next entered business, failed, and spent seventeen years of his life paying up the debts of a worthless partner. He was in love with a beautiful woman to whom he became engaged, then she died. Later he married a woman who was a constant burden to him. Entering politics again, he ran for Congress and again was badly defeated. He became a candidate for the US Senate and lost again. In 1856, he became a candidate for the vice presidency and was once more defeated. In 1856, he was defeated by Douglas.

One failure after another, bad failures, great setbacks. In the face of all this, he eventually became one of the greatest men in America, a man whose memory is honored throughout the world. When you contemplate the effect of a series of setbacks like that, does it not make you feel rather small to become discouraged?

# LIFE MESSAGE 15

## *Love Endures All Things*

There are all sorts of humorous, as well as serious, sayings about endurance. I'm sure you have heard the one so often used by the late Vince Lombardi, "Winners never quit and quitters never win."

Another football coach, Frank Lee, said, "When the going gets tough, let the tough get going."

On one occasion, a preacher was asked by an evangelist how his endurance quotient was concerning his church. The pastor said, "Not too well, brother."

The evangelist asked, "Why not?"

"Because my church is an active church," replied the preacher.

The evangelist scratched his head and tried to figure out how it could be difficult to endure an active church.

The pastor explained, "It's this way. Half of my congregation is active for me, and the other half is active against me! And that's hard to endure at times."

There's the story of the optimistic frog put in poetic structure:

Two frogs fell deep into a cream bowl.
One was an optimistic soul;
But the other took the gloomy view.
We shall drown he cried, without more ado.
So with a last despairing cry
He flung up his legs and he said good-bye.
Quote the other frog with a merry grin:
"I can't get out, but I won't give in;
I'll just swim around till my strength is spent;
Then I will die the more content."
Bravely he swam till it would seem;
His troubles began to churn the cream.
On the top of butter at last he stopped;
And out of the bowl he easily hopped.
What of the moral? Tis easily found;
If you can't hop out, keep swimming around.

Of course, endurance is a serious business. I think of our forefathers who crossed the continent on foot in pioneer days. One thing alone got them across: endurance. They traveled day after day, mile after mile, through the barrenness of the desert, the roughness of hills, all the seemingly insurmountable obstacles. What got them to their destination? It was not genius, personality, or talent, but simply endurance. That is why one of the greatest mottos of the preachers in those days was "Lord, give us a through trip." A through trip, that meant, of course, get us through.

Today, life is a rough journey for many people. They feel overwhelmed by the waves of difficulty. They hurt from many wounds, and they want to give up. The winds of resistance leave them without a breath of air.

What does God say about this? The answer is 1 Corinthians 13:7: "Love endures all things." From this marvelous vantage point, we can get new strength, courage, and dynamic to revolutionize our lives. Why? Notice, first of all, the test of love. Second, the tenacity of love, and third, the triumph of love.

## I. The Test of Love

With regard to the test of love, consider, for example, the matter of your family life. Through persecution, Jesus warned, "And brother will deliver up brother to death, and a father his child; and the children will rise up against parents, and cause them to be put to death. Do not think that I came to bring peace on earth; I did not come to bring peace, but a sword. For I came to set a man against his father, and a daughter against her mother, and a daughter-in-law against her mother-in-law and a man's enemies will be the members of his (own) household. He who loves father, mother more than Me is not worthy of Me" (Matt. 10:21, 34–37).

If we do not believe these words, we will never pass the test or love. The test of love means loving Christ supremely so that I am willing to lose my father, mother, husband, wife, sister, brother, son, daughter, or anyone else. This does not necessarily mean that a man will have to lose his wife physically. But it does mean we cannot allow a human relationship to block what we know is the will of God for us. Too often we passively allow the ones who are closest to us to divert us from following Christ. We cannot let their pressure hold us back from serving Jesus and loving Him. We must endure whatever pressure they put upon us in their efforts to keep us from living for God. Sometimes, of course, our loved ones can be used by the Lord to correct us where we are wrong. Love would dictate that we know the difference. But if we are faultless, and we are still being pressured by a loved one, we must learn to love Jesus supremely.

For example, if a girl finds love for a fellow, and he does not love Jesus supremely, if she continues to love him, she is not worthy of Jesus. That is a test she must pass. It is not worth even dating a fellow or a girl who is unsaved. Even more, do not even date someone who does not win souls. What about winning an unsaved girlfriend or boyfriend to Christ? God can use many other means to bring them to Christ.

What about the fear of man? There is a test of love in the family life also because of the fear of man. "And you will be hated by all on account of My Name, but it is the one who has endured it to the end who will be saved. And do not fear those that kill the body, but are unable to kill the soul; but rather fear Him who is able to destroy both soul and body in hell" (Matt. 10:22–23).

There is a common error abroad today. It is the belief that a Christian should not fear God, but only revere or respect Him, and that only unsaved people should fear God with trembling. The scripture does not teach that. Jesus said we are to fear Him who can cast our soul into hell. That refers to professing Christians, as well as out right unbelievers.

In Acts 5, we find the account of the lie and punishment of Ananias and Sapphira. They were Christians, not unbelievers. But they lied to the Holy Spirit, and as a result, they were both chastised to the point of physical death, in the presence of other people who faltered. Notice as a result of this: "And as he heard these words, Ananias fell down, and breathed his last; and great fear came down upon all who heard of it" (v. 5). Not just the ones who witnessed it. After the death of Sapphira, "great fear came upon the whole church" (v. 11). Great fear does come upon a church and believers. May God help us to have that same kind of fear. After Ananias and Sapphira died so suddenly, fear also came upon the unbelievers. A church that truly fears the Lord will not only influence and purify its own members, it will also influence the community. If a person does not fear God, he will fear man. He will fear circumstance.

He will fear himself, his wife, and his boss. Such people are stunted, hampered, frustrated, and they are miserable. They would not be bound by the snare of fear if they truly feared God. They would have liberty and power in their lives.

Love is also tested by the temptation to quit. Matthew 10:22 gives a wonderful assurance to the Christian who trusts in Christ. "Let him who stands take heed lest he fall." Until the day we die, we should be diligent about our salvation. The one who has endured to the end will be saved. That does not rob us of eternal security, the assurance, but it does mean this: it means that the person who is really saved, who has eternal life in Him, will live every day of his life to the end. If he does not live out his new life in Christ, he ought to question whether or not he was ever truly saved.

Some people have the idea that if they do not really stand true to Jesus at a time of persecution, surely God will understand. Beloved, no, He will not. They can plan on going to hell if they think they can deny Christ at the threat of physical death. Jesus warns us, "Take heed; behold I have told you everything in advance. Take heed, keep on the alert, for you do not know when the appointed time is. Therefore be on the alert, for you do not know whether the master of the house is coming, whether in the evening, at midnight, or cockcrowing, or in the morning, lest he come suddenly and find you asleep. And what I say to you, I say to all, 'Be on the alert!'" (Mark 13:23, 33, 35–37). A Christian who obeys this will never have any worry about trusting Christ and being true to Him when facing death, or any other trial.

Love is tested also in the matter of our self-discipline. Paul declares in 1 Corinthians 4:2, "In this case, moreover, it is required of stewards (that is, every Christian) that one be found trustworthy (or faithful!)." Note his words also in 2 Timothy 4:2: "Be urgent in season and out of season."

Christians should be characterized by faithfulness in giving out the Word of God to their neighbors, relatives, and friends. It should be their number 1 priority and their supreme love. It proves their *love* for Jesus. But many Christians fail this test of love. They do not *love* other people, and they are not faithful in witnessing. Churches have problems getting people to learn how to win souls. If a Christian is undisciplined in this, he is failing the test of love.

Look also at the matter of enduring hardness. Christians are to endure hardship as good soldiers of Jesus Christ (2 Timothy 2:3). Instead of complaining when hardships come, they should stand ready to endure them. Christians are supposed to endure joyfully (James 1:2). We are to praise God because hardship is the stuff out of which our Christian lives are made.

Note this aspect of love in 2 Thessalonians 1:4: "Therefore, we ourselves, speak proudly of you among the churches of God for your perseverance and faith in the midst of all your persecutions and afflictions when you endure." It is the mark of a true mature Christian that he stands strong in the face of all his hardships. He even says, "God, thanks for the compliment of all these problems, hardships, sufferings, persecutions and tribulations because you must think an awful lot of my strength to endure it to give it to me. And if you want to, God, give me more." That is Christ in you, beloved. That is what the love of Christ is all about.

The Athenians in their games had a very special kind of race. Those who won the crowns in the race were not necessarily the fastest, but those who endured. They gathered torches, and the winners finished with their torches still burning. This typifies Christians who, when they go through problems and pressures, wear the fire and glow of the love of God in their faces. You see them smiling the more intense it gets. That torch of the Christian in trial is the smile that reflects a deep-down joy of the love of God.

## II. The Tenacity of Love

Next, consider the matter of the tenacity of love. I just have three things to say about this: a paragraph, a portrayal, and a point.

### *A. The Paragraph*

The paragraph is simply this. The word *tenacity* means strength, and the strength of love is endurance. Why? Because in the easy things of life anybody—unsaved, carnal, or whatever—can be loving. It is only when the rough things come that the storehouse of love of God can be unlocked and opened. It floods out to show other people just what is in you.

### *B. The Portrayal*

The portrayal is of a soldier. During the Civil War, he walked from Manchester to Gettysburg. The toughest thing was not the battle itself, but rather that march of thirty-four miles. He said it was the most difficult thing he ever faced in his life. He walked through clouds of dust, mile after mile, seeing men with stubs for hands and crutches of legs, seeing cowards dropping off, seeing others wanting to turn back if someone would get the ball rolling. All these things were so difficult. He said the one thing he needed was endurance. That was the inspiration of a few that kept the others going. They were not going to quit.

More Christians should be emulative of this, Christians who will be tenacious at witnessing and at holy living. Take it a day at a time. I do not know how to live a holy life, but I can grasp living a holy day. I can take that much. That is all God expects of me, for Jesus said, "Daily bear your cross."

That is the ultimate characteristic of love. This means enduring, not simply with a passive indifference. "I'll just endure my lot in life. Poor me! If you only knew how bad I had it. If you only knew the cross I had to bear. What will be will be." Enduring love is an active, victorious, triumphant attitude. Confident of victory, the Christian sticks it out until the end. That is what endurance is.

### III. The Triumph of Love

That leads to the triumph of love. There are two kinds of people: those who allow circumstances to make them and those who make their own circumstances by the grace of God, into His synergy, power, and love. So make your circumstances. "I can't win souls. Poor me!" Make yourself win souls. "I can't be at evening service." Make yourself be at evening service.

Realize also that when all else fails, love abides. No one really knows how precious love is until all of life has caved in.

That happened to Eileen Guder in the fall of 1966. She and her husband anticipated a golden opportunity in business. The children were raised. The expenses of their college education were behind them. They looked forward to some freedom from bills and pressures. But her husband got sick, and it was diagnosed as leukemia. The night he died, the rain-soaked ceiling fell on her, literally. She saw the falling of the ceiling as only the echo of the spiritual hammer blow of her husband's death.

How did she react? "How could God do that to me? How could a loving God do this to a person like me?" No! She said, "Sickness and even death are not really the stuff that real life is made of. For God used that to show me that the real stuff out of which life is made is love, that strengthens you to endure at a time like that." She then realized her mission was to share such reality with millions of people through her writings and her lectures.

## Application

As a result of this teaching about the endurance of love, you can do only one of two things, become bitter or better. That is your choice. What shall it be?

There is an anonymous poem called "Don't Quit."

When things go wrong as they sometimes will;
When the road you're trudging seems all uphill;
When funds are low and debts are high;
And you want to smile but you have to sigh.
When care is pressing you down a bit;
Rest if you must, but don't you quit.
Life is queer with its twists and turns;
As everyone of us sometimes learns.
And many a failure turns about;
When he might have won if he stuck it out.
Don't give up though the pace seems slow;
You may succeed with another blow.
Often the goal is nearer than it seems;
To a faint and faltering man.
Often the struggler has given up;
When the might have captured the victor's cup.
And he learned too late
When the night slipped down;
How close he was to the Golden Crown.
Success is a failure turned inside out;
The silver tint of the clouds of doubt.
And you can never tell how close you are;

It may be near when it seems afar.
So stick to the fight when you're hardest hit;
It's when things seem worse that you mustn't quit.

# LIFE MESSAGE 16

## *Love Never Fails*

The Upper Room was used on more than one occasion. One of the most important occasions was when our Lord taught what is called the Upper Room Discourse (John 13–17). He shared all His plans with His disciples. If there was ever a man who had goals in life, it was Jesus Christ, and He was not afraid to share them with His followers.

Among other things, Jesus said to His troubled disciples, "Greater things shall you do than I have already done because I go to the Father" (John 14:12). I've often wondered what really was in their minds when they heard Him say those words. Greater works? Probably they would have been glad enough to do the same kind of works, or even a little bit less, than what Christ had done. But He said, "greater works." Many of them. Of course, as we know, those very apostles later on raised the dead, healed the sick, cured the blind, and preached to great crowds.

But the truths Jesus taught in the Upper Room were not just meant for the apostles; they were also meant for us today. However, I do not see Christians raising people from the dead. I do not see multitudes flocking to become Christians.

The big question comes, why? Is it a lack of faith? Or did Jesus Christ expect this only of the apostles? If this promise is only for them, we have a problem because other truths in the same discourse obviously refer to all believers. For example, heaven. "Let not your heart be troubled, you believe in God believe also in Me. In My Father's house are many mansions. If it were not so, I would have told you. And I go to pre pare a place for you" (John 14:1–3). Surely heaven is not just for the apostles.

The answer is that the "greater works" just could not include only miracles but something else as well. Perhaps something even greater than raising people from the dead. After a person is raised from the dead, he's got to live for a period of time. If he does not have something to live for, what good is being raised from the dead? After a person is healed from a sickness what good is it if he cannot have love, joy, and peace in his life? So what is greater than healing? Jesus reached the climax of all those "greater works" when He said, "Greater love has no man than this, that a man lay down his life for his friends" (John 15:13). That is the greatest work, love. That is what the Apostle Paul describes in 1 Corinthians 13.

In this chapter, we want to see the absolute supremacy of love. Paul proves this supremacy by three facts: the partial is to be done away (vv. 8–10); the process is to be done away (v. 11); and the perfect is here to stay (v. 12).

## I. The Partial Is to Be Done Away

Paul says, "We know in part, and we prophesy in part, but when the perfect comes the partial will be done away." What does he mean?

### *A. The Place of the Partial*

He explains in Ephesians 2:20–21, "Having been built upon the foundation of the apostles and prophets Christ Jesus Himself being the corner stone, in whom the whole building being fitted together is growing into a holy temple in the Lord." Paul refers not to a building of brick and mortar and stone, but rather the church, the individual members who make up the body of Christ. The church is a building made up of spiritual stones.

Notice the foundation is already done. It stands firm so we can rely upon it and build upon it, knowing it will not crumble beneath us.

Christ is not referred to here as the foundation in the church. Paul says the apostles and prophets are the foundation and Christ Himself is the cornerstone. The ministry of the apostles and the New Testament prophets is what Paul means by "the partial." They spoke the Word in prophecy because there was no written New Testament, they got knowledge fresh from heaven, and they even spoke in tongues. These were the things by which the apostles and prophets laid the foundation of the church.

### *B. The Period of the Partial*

Their miracles, their greater works were the foundation. There was a reason for that. Whenever God did an unusual work, He blessed certain messengers, whether they were prophets or apostles, with unusual gifts to perform miracles. This was so that when they preached the message of God, people would believe them, if for no other reason than the miraculous works. There were three great periods of miracles.

One was during the time of Moses. Moses needed miracles to confirm his message to the Pharaoh because the Pharaoh would not change his mind.

The second period of miracles was when Elijah and Elisha had to revive Israel. During that period of time, there was a great outpouring of miracles.

The third period of time was the time of Christ that included the apostles and New Testament prophets. All of these miraculous works, raising the dead, healing people, speaking in tongues, prophecies, special revelations from heaven, were done at the foundation. Why? Because God was about to initiate another work, the work of the church. In order to establish it in the eyes of the people, and give it credibility, miracles were necessary.

*C. The Purpose of the Partial*

Notice, however, that "the partial will be done away." *The partial* refers back to verse 9, "For we know in part and prophesy in part." Why the partial must "be done away" is because you do not keep building a foundation. There comes a time when you stop building a foundation, you build the superstructure, and ingredients that go into the foundation do not go into the superstructure.

This refers not only to the foundational gifts of the apostles and prophets but also to all the gifts listed in 1 Corinthians 12–14. When God brings about a new heaven and a new earth, we will not need any one of the eighteen or more gifts mentioned. Even those gifts in a sense are partial. But Paul says "the perfect" is coming, and it will remain forever and ever. What is the "perfect"?

## II. The Process Is to Be Done Away

In verse 2, Paul speaks about a child. He does so because he wants to illustrate the necessity of love. He illustrates what we are to be doing during the time between the foundation of the church and the coming of the kingdom. He calls this a period of childhood. In other words, Christians are to grow up and put away childish things. "When I was a child, I used to speak as a child, think as a child, reason as a child."

These verbs—*speak*, *think*, *reason*—are directly parallel to speaking in tongues, the gift of prophesy, and the gift of knowledge. These three "childish" ways of behavior are compared to three spiritual gifts that went into the foundation of the church. The child referred to here in verse 11 is the church. Beyond Paul's own testimony, there is a figure of speech. He represents the whole church. The church is supposed to be putting away childish things.

### *A. Speaking as a Child*

What is the implication? Tongues are the baby talk of the church, not the adult talk. How do I know? Because the word *child* is not the word for a boy of growing age, say from six to twelve; it is the word for baby, infant. How does an infant talk? "Da-da, goo-goo, gege." It does not make sense. That is how Paul describes tongues. How does a baby talk? Out of turn, many times. You see that in tongues.

Baby talk is cute, but it is certainly not a sign of maturity. It certainly is not edifying.

In 1 Corinthians 14:18–19, Paul says, "I thank God, I speak in tongues more than you all. However, in the church I desire to speak five words in my mind, that I may instruct others also, rather than ten thousand words in a tongue." By AD 50 or

55 at the latest, Paul was already putting away tongues, putting away "the baby talk." Paul also commanded, "Be imitators of me just as I am of Christ" (1 Corin. 11:1). I get the impression that Paul was saying, "You put away the baby talk too."

*B. Thinking as a Child*

Let us move on to the next one: "Think as a child." What else did Paul put away? "Thinking," or prophecy. You must think to talk correctly; you must think to be able to preach, to prophesize, especially to convey some revelation that God gives you on the spot. Direct revelation through a messenger to people is prophecy. But according to Paul, that was the baby thought of the early church. Think about a baby. A baby doesn't think for itself; a baby depends on the thinking of its parents. A baby is helpless and cannot think in terms of helping itself. That is what is meant here.

The Apostle John explains in Revelation 22:18–19:

> I testify to everyone who hears the words of the prophecy of this book; if anyone adds to them, God shall add to him the plagues which are written in this book; if anyone takes away from the words of the book of this prophecy, God shall take away his part from the tree of life and from the holy city, which are written in this book.

The last book of the Bible was written by the end of the first century.

Therefore, there is no more revelation coming to us in the character of prophecy, as it did in the infant church.

### *C. Reasoning as a Child*

Paul's next phrase is "Reason as a child." How does a child reason? The reasoning is self-centered and self-excusing. Sometimes children are logical, but most of the time they are unconvincing and inconclusive. Paul compares this to the gift of knowledge in the early church.

If a person doesn't have a Bible, he needs a special kind of knowledge that comes directly from God. The early Christians needed that during the time, but we are not in that kind of situation. We have the complete Bible. We are mature in the sense we have full knowledge of God in His Word. We need nothing else. We do not have to say, "I wish God would tap me on the shoulder." That is baby reasoning. The answer is in the scripture. Paul says when he became a man, he put away childish things. So should we.

Paul exhorts in Philippians 2:12–13, "So, then, my beloved, just as you have always obeyed, not as in my presence only, but now much more in my absence, work out your salvation with fear and trembling; for it is God who is at work in you, both to will and to work for His good pleasure." Even when Paul was not present, he expected the Philippians to follow him. He is not around today, but we should still follow him, in terms of the scripture.

God is at work in us, willing to do and to work for His good pleasure.

So we have the power to do so. Every Christian can walk on his own two feet. There is no need to talk baby talk, to think baby thoughts, and to reason as a baby.

## III. The Perfect Is Here to Stay

Sir Isaac Newton, just before his death, made this remark: "I do not know what I appear to the world, but to myself I seem to have been only like a boy playing on the seashore and diverting myself now and then finding a smoother pebble or a prettier shell than the ordinary, while the great ocean of truth lay all undiscovered before me."

We can move on to something more than that because we have the power in Christ, a power greater than the creative power Newton had. The key is found in 1 Corinthians 13:12, "For now we see in that mirror dimly."

### *A. Not the Medium of Knowing*

The word *mirror* translated can mean either a mirror or a window. In the original Greek, the preposition *in* is not used; it is the word *through*. I think a better translation is this: "For now we see through a window dimly."

"The most natural idea is that of seeing objects by an imperfect medium," said Pliny, the ancient philosopher and scholar, "by looking through something in contemplating them." It is, therefore, probable that Paul refers to those transparent substances, which the ancients had and which they had used in their windows occasionally such as thin slates of horn, transparent stone, etc. Windows were often made by lapis specularis, which was pellucid and was split into thin laminae or scales, probably the same as mica.

It is not, therefore, unlikely that such material was used in Paul's day. Paul is describing people inside the house looking out the window. It was not a clear transparent window such as we have. It was like frosted glass, but they could still see the figures of people outside. However, they could not tell for sure who the person was coming to the house. That fits the context here better than *mirror* because you cannot see through a mirror. The point is, we don't see through a window like that. We can see face to face, just like you see a friend face to face, and see him clearly.

*B. But the Reality of Knowledge*

The word *know* is the word that refers not to theoretical knowledge but to experiential knowledge. Added to that experiential knowledge is the idea of being fully known and knowing fully. It is the word for such an intimate knowledge of a person that it is used to describe the experience of Isaac and Rebecca on their wedding night.

The Bible says, "And he knew her." Paul says love never ends, so one day we shall know even as we are fully known by God already. God describes our knowing Him and His knowing us as the result of unfailing love.

**Application**

We are to respond to this truth by growing up. Whatever gifts we have, let us use them. Let us not emphasize the foundational ones. Some people still persist in baby stuff. As for me, I do not need baby talk, baby thought, and baby reasoning. I want to build a superstructure, not a foundation. The foundation is finished. I want to stand upon it, and I want to build upon it with preaching, teaching, prayer, and faith. Even all these gifts will be put away one day, and by the grace of God, the one thing that is going to last for eternity is love. As I am growing up, I want to love people, really love them, and I want them to love me. I want to know God as He knows me.

That is Christian maturity. May you have it.

# LIFE MESSAGE 17

## *Love Is the Greatest*

Gift, estate, and income taxes have not significantly decreased the financial tide going to the rich, says a report by the Carnegie Institute. On the other hand, welfare, social security, and other payments from the government to the poorest one-fifth of the people have not caused any significant improvement in their financial situation.

The institute, which specializes in social research, concludes that there has not been any significant redistribution of either income or wealth in the US for the last generation. Other findings in the report include,

1. The dollar-gap between the richest and poorest one-fifth of the population is increasing.
2. Some 45 percent of all salaried income, which goes to the top one-fifth of the population, is increasing.
3. Over 60 percent of income from personal businesses and property goes to the highest one-fifth.
4. The top one-fifth owns 77 percent of total personal wealth.
5. One percent of Americans own between 20 and 30 percent of all personal wealth.

6. Only 5 percent of the population reports a substantial inheritance; however of those whose wealth is over $500,000, 34 percent report a substantial inheritance.
7. From 1950 to 1970, the bottom one-fifth's share of total personal income rose only 1 percent, from 4.5 percent to 5.5 percent.
8. In 1968, the average family in the poorest one-fifth had an annual income of $3,085 per year while the average income for a family in the highest one-fifth was $21,973 per year.

When you see statistics like that, you become convinced that money is a problem. If they tell us nothing else, they show that the greatest nation cannot solve money problems.

**I. It Is Not Money**

This is one reason we are told by God that money is not the greatest investment we will ever make in life. This chapter is about the greatest investment you will ever make. The first point simply is, it is not money. But why not?

In Matthew 6:19–20, Jesus says,

> Do not lay up for yourselves treasures upon earth, where moth and rust destroy, and where thieves break in and steal. But lay up for yourselves treasures in heaven, where neither moth nor rust destroys, and where thieves do not break in and steal.

Notice also verse 24,

> No one can serve two masters; for either he will hate the one and serve the other, or he

> will hold to one and despise the other. You cannot serve God and mammon (money).

What does money have to do with a book on love? Very much because although people in general are willing to say love is the greatest investment they can ever make, in truth men serve and love money far more than they serve or love God, or love. It is serving the "almighty buck" instead of the almighty God. That is really where America stands as a nation today.

It is very important to get this point clearly in mind in order to understand what really is the greatest investment we can make in life.

We are all a part of this society in which the pursuit of money is so prevalent. We are unable to clearly appreciate what love is really all about unless we first remove whatever cobwebs are in our thinking with regard to money.

Is money really bad? No, money in itself is good. Money is a wonderful thing. It is a convenient, efficient medium of exchange. It represents power, but so often it is used for wrong goals. That is why Paul told Timothy to spread the word throughout the churches that the love of money is the root of all evil. That is why we should not make money our greatest investment in life. Even if there were not so many evils in the misuse of money, it would still not be the greatest investment you could ever make because even properly used money is subject to moths and rust that destroy, and the thieves that break in and steal. Even if those things were not a threat to your money, one day your money will completely disappear, and in your eternal state, the only currency will be the money of love.

A financial investment is certainly not the greatest investment you can ever make, and yet how hard it is for people to learn that lesson well. Practically, we have a problem. The rich man in the story told by Jesus said to himself, "Soul, you have many goods laid up for many years to come; take your ease, eat, drink, and be merry. But God said to him, "You fool, this very night your soul is required of you; and now who will own what you have prepared?" (Luke 12:19–20).

## II. It Is Not Humanitarianism

Would to God we could learn that lesson. Would to God that we could also realize that the greatest investment in life is not humanitarianism.

### A. Whether It Is for Family

Erotic love in its proper perspective is wonderful in the bond of matrimony and family. But as wonderful and powerful as it is, it is not the same as the Christian love spoken of in 1 Corinthians 13. Romantic love cannot compare to Christian love, neither can a man's love for his wife or children. The love of a man for his wife and children, which causes him to give his life for them and which causes him to dedicate his whole being to their provision, protection, and preservation, as great as all that is, is not Christian love.

### B. Whether It Be for Friends

May I go a step further? The love spoken of in this chapter is greater than the love of a friend for his friend. No matter how great a friend's love may be for his other friends, it cannot compare to Christian love. A man can love a friend so much that he'll die in his place, but that still is not the love spoken of in 1 Corinthians 13. That is why the apostle says, "Though I give my body to be burned and give all my possessions to feed the poor, but have not love, it profits me nothing."

C. Whether It Be for Strangers

There is also philanthropic love that embraces strangers, the poor, and the needy. If we provide for them and care for them to the point of giving up all we own, even our very lives, even that is not the love spoken of in this chapter. Such love is not the greatest investment a person can make. Humanitarianism in the world, no matter how great it might be, is not love as the Bible speaks of it here. Therefore, it cannot be considered the greatest investment you can ever make. If it is not money, it is not humanitarianism, then what is it?

**III. It Is Love**

Having considered what the best investment is not, let us consider what the best investment is. What is it? "But now abide faith, hope, love, these three; but the greatest of these is love." The greatest investment we can ever make in life is the love of God. It is so great that even faith and hope cannot be compared to it. Love surpasses all that went into the foundation of the church, all the miracles of raising the dead, healing the blind and the sick, speaking in tongues, and all the other miraculous gifts. All the gifts of preaching and teaching are not to be considered the greatest investment in life. Even sharing Christ with someone else is not the greatest investment. No, it is love, self-giving love.

To define love once more; it is what you do to someone else without any thought of return. It is what you give to someone without any consideration whether they deserve it or not. It is unconditional in character. It is all-inclusive. It is giving your life for people for their highest good and for God's highest glory. That is love. That is the only thing in this world worth investing in. Why? Because it is the only thing that will last beyond death.

Look at the text: "But now abide faith." Now, the present time. Even faith and hope are now. We will use them and they are great to invest in now, but even faith and hope will not go beyond the grave. Why?

Look at verse 7: Love is so fulfilling, so self-containing, and so complete and central that it has all it needs within itself. Love is everything, absolutely, and it will even carry us through eternity. It is the atmosphere of heaven as well as the currency for earth for the believer in Christ.

**Application**

Augustine had it right when he said this: "Love is so inclusive that it even takes the four cardinal virtues of Greek philosophy and supersedes them as well as fulfills them. Temperance, fortitude, justice and prudence." Temperance is nothing more than love keeping itself entire and uncorrupted for God. Fortitude is nothing but love bearing readily everything for the sake of God. Justice is serving God only and therefore fulfilling well all else as subject to men. Prudence is love making a right distinction between what helps it toward God and hinders it from God. Love even fulfills faith because love hopes all things.

In the days of Archibald Rutledge, a preacher died, but his widow kept on serving people, helping the poor, nursing the orphans, helping other widows. Archibald Rutledge was so pleased and thrilled with this widow's service for the Lord that he built her a beautiful home in his own backyard. The first day it was open, she invited the most disreputable woman of the community. Rutledge took her aside and said, "What did you do that for? Why did you have this woman in your home on my property?"

Her answer was "Jesus would, that's why!"

Our hearts agree with the answer, Jesus would. Jesus would.

That is just like Jesus, that is unconditional love, the only thing worth investing in for time and eternity.

# PART 3

## *God's Exemplification of Love*

The disciples are gathered around the Lord Jesus, listening to Him teach the Upper Room Discourse (John 13–16). One of the most important truths he taught was this: "Greater love has no man than this, that he lay down his life for his friends." What love that is, that would actually drive a person to give his life for someone else.

Such love is applied love. Such love is love in action. But the question comes, how did the disciples who learned this truth apply it? What record do we have in God's Word that shows just what these men did?

In the book of Acts, we find that God has given just such a record. Luke writes, "The first account I composed, Theophilus, about all that Jesus began to do and teach" (Acts 1:1). The link between the Upper Room teaching and how the disciples applied it later is found in the word *began*. Luke was the author of both the gospel of Luke and the book of Acts. Referring to his gospel, he says it simply is what Jesus Christ began to do and teach. In the gospel of Luke, we see Christ doing and teaching in His earthly body, whereas in Acts, we see what He does and teaches from the Father's right hand, in His glorified body, through His disciples. In the book of Acts, we see the unfolding of the obedience of the earthly disciples to the teachings of Christ.

For that reason, I have chosen to use this book to review the seventeen characteristics of love as we have already discussed.

Notice in 1 Corinthians 13 that there are three dimensions of love: negative, positive, and superlative. There are eight characteristics of love in the negative, indicating what love is not. Love is not jealous, boastful, arrogant, discourteous, selfish, provoked, unforgiving, or unseemly. Then there are seven characteristics of love in the positive; love is patient, kind, rejoicing, responsible, believing, optimistic, and enduring.

In the third place, there are some superlatives about love in 1 Corinthians 13:8 and 13. It never ends and it is the greatest. Now consider the book of Acts and see how the disciples applied all of these dimensions of love.

## I. The Negative Dimension

### *A. Love Is Not Jealous (2:14)*

"But Peter, taking his stand with the eleven, raised his voice and declared to them: 'Men of Judea, and all of you who live in Jerusalem, let this be known to you and give heed to my words."

The day the church began, there were eleven other apostles with Peter as he preached. But there was not a trace of jealousy. That was love in action. They all were not preaching, although the others had listened to Jesus Christ teach in His earthly life. Only one did the preaching. Note how it is described: "taking his stand with the eleven, he raised his voice." The rest, I'm sure, were praying, supporting, and loving. They were not jealous.

### *B. Love Is Not Boastful (3:11–13)*

"And while he was clinging to Peter and John, all the people ran together to them at the so-called portico of Solomon, full of amazement. But when Peter saw this, he replied to the people, Men of Israel, why do you marvel at this, or why do you gaze at us, as if by our own power or piety we have made him walk? The God of Abraham, Isaac, and Jacob, the God of our fathers, has glorified His Servant Jesus, the one whom you delivered up."

Peter made the point that he had not done a thing, that John had not done a thing, that none of the apostles had done a thing in the healing of this man. They gave glory to God. They boasted in the grace of God, if they boasted at all. Love did not boast in this case because they gave God the glory for the great things He had done.

### *C. Love Is Not Arrogant (4:13)*

"Now as they observed the confidence of Peter and John and understood that they were uneducated and untrained men, they were marveling and began to recognize them as having been with Jesus." The power of the love of God in Christ did not puff up these men with pride or arrogance, but rather it enabled people to see Jesus puffed up in them, so to speak. That was true, even in the midst of the great works done by these men.

### *D. Love Is Not Discourteous (5:40–41)*

"And they took Gamaliel's advice and after calling the apostles in, they flogged them and ordered them to speak no more in the name of Jesus, and they released them." The occasion for such flogging was the evangelism by the Christians in Jerusalem. The response of the apostles to the flogging is what we want to see in verse 41: "So they went on their way from the presence of the Council, rejoicing that they had been considered worthy to suffer shame for His Name." Being so positively absorbed in rejoicing, and in considering it a privilege to suffer for Jesus, there was no chance for any sort of discourtesy.

*E. Love Is Not Selfish (6:37)*

"But select from among you, brethren, seven men of good reputation, full of the Spirit and of wisdom, whom we may put in charge of this task. But we will devote ourselves to prayer, and to the ministry of the word, And the statement found approval with the whole congregation." Such unselfishness really won the hearts of the whole congregation, which by this time included at least eight thousand people. Note in verse 7: "And the Word of God kept on spreading." When Christians are unselfish, the Word of God spreads. That is an unfailing law. When Christians stop being selfish, the church increases.

*F. Love Is Not Provoked (15:37)*

"And Barnabas was desirous of taking John, called Mark, along with them also. But Paul kept insisting that they should not take him along who deserted them in Pamphylia and had not gone with them to the work, And there arose such a sharp disagreement." Even in the early church, men disagreed. The disagreement was so bad that Barnabas took Mark and went on to Cyprus while Paul went a different way with Silas. The reason for the disagreement was that Paul was not loving in this case. Paul was provoked with John Mark. On the first missionary journey, he turned back and went home. But does that mean that the Apostle Paul should have held it against him? Note what finally happened because Barnabas loved John Mark and gave him another chance. In 2 Timothy 4:11, Paul says, "Only Luke is with me. Pick up Mark and bring him with you, for he is useful to me for service." Thanks to the love of Barnabas, John Mark was redeemed for the Lord's service. This is a lesson to learn.

*G. Love Is Not Unforgiving (16:19–25)*

"But when her masters saw that their hope of profit was gone, they seized Paul and Silas and dragged them into the market place before the authorities, and when they had brought them to the chief magistrates, they said, These men are throwing our city into confusion, being Jews, and are proclaiming customs. And when they had inflicted many blows upon them, they threw them into prison, commanding the jailer to guard them securely; and he, having received such a command, threw them into the inner prison, and fastened their feet ill stocks."

Did Paul and Silas demand their rights? As a result of such treatment, did they cry for revenge? No! "But about midnight Paul and Silas were praying and singing hymns to God." The next time you are unjustly treated, do what Paul and Silas did—pray, praise God, and leave any kind of retribution to Him. Do not try to justify yourself; do not try to get even.

*H. Love Is Not Unseemly (16:26–34)*

After the earthquake, "immediately all the doors were opened and everyone's chains were unfastened. And when the jailer had been roused out of his sleep and had seen the prison doors opened, he drew his sword and was about to kill himself, supposing that the prisoners had escaped. But Paul cried out with a loud voice, 'Do yourself no harm, for we are all here!' And he called for lights and rushing in and, trembling with fear, he fell down before Paul and Silas. And after he brought them out, he said, 'Sirs, what must I do to be saved?" When we learn to be so loving to people that we do not even laugh inside when they are wrong, and hurt, and harmed, they will leap out of the kingdom of darkness and beg us to show them the way to salvation. Love does find a way.

When we exert our self-control in our actions, endeavoring to be loving, people get saved, even through our lives.

### *I. Love Never Acts Like a Failure (16:35; 17:9)*

In this passage, we see the officials at Philippi begging Paul and Silas to leave the city because they discovered they were Roman citizens.

But they did not fail to fulfill their ministry before they left. Paul and Silas, with sorely beaten backs, rebuked the chief magistrates by their boldness. They left the prison, but not as yet the city. Because love never fails, they went to the believers in the city and strengthened them in their faith. Finally, they departed but only to go on to Thessalonica where they kept on ministering the Word of God. What a portrayal of love never failing in such indefatigable men of God!

## II. The Positive Dimension

Now we pass on to the positive dimension of love.

### *A. Love Is Patient (18:24)*

"Now a certain Jew named Apollos, all Alexandrian by birth, all eloquent man, came to Ephesus; and he was mighty in the Scriptures. This man had been instructed in the way of the Lord; and being fervent in spirit, he was speaking and teaching accurately the things concerning Jesus, being acquainted only with the baptism of John." Apollos was limited in his teaching. As a result, Priscilla and Aquila "took him aside and explained the way of God more accurately." The key phrase is "they took him aside" and in patience and love showed him the more accurate way.

How love works! Note the effect it had upon him: "And when he wanted to go across to Achaia, the brethren encouraged him and wrote to the disciples to welcome him; and when he had arrived, he helped greatly those who had believed through grace; for he powerfully refuted the Jews in public, demonstrating by the Scriptures that Jesus was the Christ." Apollos could preach that way, thanks to loving, gracious, patient Priscilla and Aquila.

*B. Love Is Kind (20:7)*

"And on the first day of the week, when we were gathered together to break bread, Paul began talking to them, intending to depart the next day, and he prolonged his message until midnight." The first act of kindness here is the congregation. They let Paul preach until midnight. Only a kind congregation will let you do that.

Second, Paul was kind. We see his kindness in what followed. A man called Eutychus fell asleep while Paul was preaching. I cannot imagine the Apostle Paul letting anyone fall asleep in his preaching.

"And there was a certain man named Eutychus sitting on a windowsill sinking into a deep sleep; and as Paul kept on talking, he was overcome by sleep and fell down from the third floor, and was picked dead. But Paul went down and fell upon him and after embracing him, he said, 'Do not be troubled, for his life is in him.' And they took away the boy alive, and were greatly comforted." Paul was upset by John Mark's failure, but this case he healed the young man. Only love can change a man like that.

*C. Love Rejoices (20:18–25)*

"And when they had come to him, he said to them, 'You yourselves know, from the first day that I set foot in Asia, how I was with you the whole time, serving the Lord with all humility and with tears and with trials which came upon me through the plots of the Jews; how I did not shrink from declaring to you anything that was profitable, and teaching you publicly and from house to house." Here is a commentary on what it means to rejoice in truth. It does not mean saying, "I am happy for my Bible and here is the reason why." It means giving out the word of truth in all kinds of persecution, and still being happy for the privilege. It means giving your all and spending yourself in every house in town. Paul did this all through the city of Ephesus, a city of five hundred thousand people. But even when the people of Asia turned against him (2 Timothy 1:15), he was practicing love. He could have recalled the words of Jesus, in the great Sermon on the Mount, that when you are persecuted for righteousness sake, you are to rejoice and be exceedingly glad. That is what rejoicing in truth means; that is part of being loving.

*D. Love Is Responsible (20:26–27)*

"Therefore I testify to you this day, that I am innocent of the blood of all men. For I did net shrink from declaring to you the whole purpose of God."

Love bears responsibility. It does not hear only the command "Reach your neighbors for Christ," and then forget.

It hears it and then does it. The Christian who does not win souls is an unloving Christian. It is not a lack of knowledge, it is not a lack of confidence, it is not a lack of gifts; it is a lack of love. If Christians take this truth and put it into action, we would see tremendous church growth.

*E. Love Is Believing (21:14)*

"And since he would not be persuaded, we fell silent, remarking, 'The will of the Lord be done!'" A person, convinced of the truth of the scriptures, finds it very difficult to watch believers grow so slowly. We get impatient with their lack of growth. However, even after we do our best to help them, we have to say with those disciples who did not convince Paul, "The will of the Lord be done." God can give us that conviction, that expression of love, after having done all we can. Once we have done that, and still there is no response, we must believe that God's will shall be done. Therefore, do your best and commit the rest.

*F. Love Is Optimistic (23:10–24)*

Paul was not persuaded by the Ephesian elders to stay away from Jerusalem. At first he was greatly welcomed by the people. He told the Christians about all the great works God had done in the difficult cities of Asia and Europe. So great was the report that the Jews found out, and the Jews maneuvered to get him arrested. They wanted to have him executed. Paul tried to defend himself before the council in Jerusalem, but such a dissension among the council members broke out that the commander of the troops was afraid for Paul's life. So he "ordered the troops to go down and take him away from them by force, and bring him back into the barracks. But on the night immediately following, the Lord stood at his side and said, 'Take courage; for as you have solemnly witnessed to my cause at Jerusalem, so you must witness at Rome also.' And when it was day, the Jews formed a conspiracy and bound themselves under an oath, saying that they would neither eat nor drink until they had killed Paul. And there were more than forty that formed this plot. And they came to the chief priests and the elders, and said, 'We have bound ourselves under a solemn oath to taste nothing until we have killed Paul.'"

Even at a time like this, love is optimistic. You don't have to worry about protecting yourself when you are secure in the love of God.

You can be a tough-minded optimist in the most antagonistic circumstances. At such times God will even get an army on your side, so to speak, as He did to rescue Paul. Paul went along like a little lamb. Why? Because he had the power of the love of God.

*G. Love Is Enduring (28:6–8)*

"And when we entered Rome, Paul was allowed to stay by himself, with the soldier who was guarding him. And it happened that after three days he called together those who were the leading men of the Jews, and when they had come together, he began saying to them, 'Brethren, though I had done nothing against our people, or the customs of our fathers, yet I was delivered prisoner from Jerusalem into the hands of the Romans. And when they had examined me, they were willing to release me because there was no ground for putting me to death.'" Paul was not released. He was in that house for two and one-half years, but oh, the people who came to Christ! Love caused Paul to endure in the proclamation of the Gospel.

## III. The Superlative Dimension (Acts 28:25)

The superlative dimension of love is our conclusion. This is in Acts 28:25–28: "The Holy Spirit rightly spoke through Isaiah the prophet to your fathers."

Paul then gives the quotation, saying, "Go to this people and say: 'You will keep on hearing, but will not understand; and you will keep on seeing, but will not perceive; for the heart of this people has become dull, and with their ears they scarcely hear, and they have closed their eyes; lest they should see with their eyes, and hear with their ears, and understand with their ears, and understand with their heart and turn again, and I should heal them.' Let it be known to you, therefore, that this nation of God has been sent to the Gentiles, they will also listen."

One thing is for certain: the Holy Spirit stayed with Paul to the very end. The love of God in Christ through Paul was lasting. In the last chapter of Acts, love is going greater than ever.

## Application (Acts 28:30–31)

"And he stayed two full years in his own rented quarters, and he was welcoming all who came to him, preaching the kingdom of God, and teaching concerning the Lord Jesus Christ with all openness, unhindered." The love of God abides; that is how the book of Acts closes. The book has no real conclusion. Why? Because the direction of the book of Acts is that the acts of love should continue through Christians today. Why? Because love not only acts as the greatest, it is the greatest!

# PART 4

## *God's Expression of Love*

The captain of a ship crossing the Atlantic said to a minister aboard, "We have just crossed over the place where the *Titanic*, the alleged unsinkable ship, went down!"

Later the minister said, "I thought of all the wreckage beyond the power of man to recover and redeem. I thought of the great bed of the deep sea, with its treasures that are too far down for man to reach and restore. Too far down!"

And then he thought of all the human wreckage there is engulfed and sunk in the depths of nameless sin. "Too far down! For what? Not too far down for the love of God!"

And yet, why is it that more people do not avail themselves of God's love? What is it about people that makes them so unbelieving about God's love? Recently someone told me, "I really don't believe that God will heal me because I'm not really convinced that He actually loves me that much."

Such a statement accurately expresses the feelings of most people. It reminds me of one morning years ago when I wanted to feed the birds. It was gray and cold, and the ground was covered with snow. I stepped out on the porch with a handful of crumbs and called to them. But they did not respond. There they sat, cold, hungry, and afraid.

They did not trust me. As I sat and watched and waited, it seemed to me that I understood God's viewpoint more clearly than ever before. He offers, He plans, He watches, He waits, He hopes, He longs for all things for our good. But He has to watch and wait, as I did for those timid birds.

Does this sound familiar? Is it possible that you don't trust God's love? Yet John 3:16 still stands. Perhaps you need to understand.

You recall the story. Nicodemus was the elderly religious man who was a ruler of the Jews. He approached Christ in the middle of the night. Why then? Probably for two reasons: l) because he wanted to speak with Christ privately and confidentially, not during the day when the crowds might have interfered with his conversation and 2) because he felt embarrassed, for he had to ask questions of Christ, the answers to which he, a prominent and religious leader, should have known.

Nicodemus had all the religion a man could offer, but not the reality of God's love inside his heart, which only Christ could offer. After Nicodemus expressed his absolute confidence in Christ, Christ responded in very direct and emphatic words, "Truly, truly, I say to you, unless one is born again, he cannot see the Kingdom of God" (3:3).

The following explanation reaches its zenith and climax in 3:16: "For God so loved the world that He gave His only begotten Son, that whoever believes in Him, should not perish, but have eternal life." Without these words, Nicodemus would have been left right where he was. But because of these words, his life was changed. Anyone's life can be changed if they are willing to go the way of this verse.

The verse opens with the expression of God's love, "For God so loved the world." The word *so* means "in such a way." In what way is that? God's answer is 1) by way of super sacrifice, 2) by way of simple surrender, and 3) by way of solid security. It is the way of super sacrifice because "He gave His only begotten Son." It is the way of simple surrender because "whoever believes in Him." It is the way of solid security because of the words "should not perish but have eternal life."

## I. Via Super Sacrifice

God loved the world, that is, the whole cosmos of men, including the Gentile and heathen, the whole human race in such a way that He gave His only begotten Son for it. That way of love goes quite far and wide. The Lord reveals love as the one ground of the divine counsel in the gift of His Son to man. What an expression of love! It was this that prompted God to give man the Savior. God's love expressed the benevolent, merciful feelings that He had for man, that He was so earnestly desirous of man's happiness. That's why *gospel* means glad tidings. To be sure, it is good news, the best and happiest in this universe!

The expression of God's love in terms of the super sacrifice of His own Son vividly reminds us of the offering of Isaac upon the altar. Abraham loved God so much that he was willing to give up his son to die on the altar of sacrifice in order to prove his love. Likewise, God loved the world in such a way that He gave up His Son to die on the altar of the cross for the sins of the world, to have His dear Son's life blood shed to wash away as well as cover the guilt of mankind. Surely Nicodemus, possibly remembering the story of Isaac, was quite impressed by the love that such a sacrifice required.

God's love is a free gift, unmerited, undeserved. He gave us His Son as an absolute gift, an unconditional gift. Man had no claim, and when there was no eye to pity, or arm to save, it pleased God to give His Son into the hands of men to die in their place. It was the expression of His eternal compassion and His desire that sinners should not perish forever.

Not only was the gift God's Son, but also God's only begotten Son. This is a very interesting term in Greek. It means "unique," one of a kind. How is He unique? Very simple, but yet profound. He was the only eternally born Son of God. Men can be the created sons of God, but only Christ is the eternally born Son of God.

That is why the gift of God's Son to the world is the highest expression of love that we can imagine. Should a parent give up his only son to die, if this could or might be done, this would show the highest love. This is how God manifested His love. This shows something of the depth of the love of God.

In St. Paul's Cathedral, London, there is a life-size marble statue of Christ writhing in anguish on the cross. The statue is inscribed "This is how God loved the world!"

Ironically, however such an expression of the love of God shows the depths of the sin of man. The sacrifice of Christ was only the means by which the redemption of man could be effected. Christ's death alone was sufficient to accomplish this gracious design. It would have been inconsistent with the wisdom of God to have appointed a sacrifice greater than itself or less in its merit than what the urgent necessities of the case required.

Consider the startling implications here. Our sin, the sin of mankind, any and all of the sins of the world, is so indescribably evil and terrible that it required no less sacrifice to make payment for it than God manifested in the flesh.

Why? Human beings by nature have a hard time believing that anyone really loved them, especially God. So by giving us His Son, God manifested His love for us. It is inescapable! God loves us. We know He does because He proved it by giving His Son. He did not just send His Son as an ambassador to negotiate peace between heaven and earth, but rather He gave up His Son to the world. Even though the Son was powerful enough to prevent anyone from taking His life, God gave it away. Nor was this done on the spur of the moment (cf. Acts 2:23). Before the world began, God the Father planned His determinate counsel to give Him up. He was slain before the foundation of the world! Before you and I were born, Christ died for us in the mind of God. Oh, what love!

Is it any wonder that Peter Mackenzie said, "There are two striking things in my text: When God loves He loves a world; when He gives, He gives a Son."

That is why fond parents say to a child, "How much do you love me?" The answer is usually a kiss and a hug. If you put the same question to our Heavenly Father, the answer is the cross!

## II. Via Simple Surrender

As great as this sacrifice was, no man is saved through this sacrifice unless he believes. He needs to surrender himself to the simple yet profound realization that God provided all that was necessary for his salvation in Christ. He must give God the credit. He must rely personally upon what God has spoken regarding Christ, His sacrifice, the end for which it was offered, and the way in which it is to be applied in order to become effectual. That is the meaning of the second part of the verse, "whoever believes in Him."

### *A. The Implication*

The *whoever* does not include angels, for the good angels do not need salvation, and yet they desire to look into what it is like. The fallen angels do not even have a chance. One-third of the angels of God fell with Lucifer, that is Satan, at the beginning, and yet none of them have ever had a chance to be saved. Man was created a little lower than the angels, and yet the fallen angels have not been included in God's offer of salvation.

In the fifth chapter of Mark, there is a very striking insight. The demon-possessed man, Legion, was called such because he had a legion of demons in him. According to the Roman Empire's measuring standard, a legion is equivalent to six thousand to twelve thousand men; it is the largest single unit of an army. Just imagine, one man is more important to God than six thousand to twelve thousand fallen angels!

On the other hand, *whoever* does not mean Jews only. The conceited Jews vainly imagined that the Messiah should be sent in love only to their nation. But God tellls us that He sent His Son in love to the whole world! Whoever in this whole world believes in Christ can be saved!

Whoever in this whole world who has revolted and rebelled against God and broken His commandments can be included in God's love. There is no sin, there is no mistake, there is no fault, there is nothing that a person has done that is so bad that it cannot be forgiven.

*B. The Condition*

All that anyone has to do to be saved from his sin is to believe. However, we must not overlook the real meaning of the word *believe*. We must not confuse it with the shallow, empty, meaningless concept that many Americans have.

When the late Donald Grey Barnhouse went to South America on a preaching tour during the latter part of his life, he was approached by a missionary who had a problem in translation. He was translating the gospel of John from the Greek into a tribal dialect. His problem was how to translate the word *believe*. The only word in the tribal dialect that was even closely equivalent to it was the word *believe obey*. The missionary was reluctant to use it because he was afraid of misleading the tribe into a doctrine of salvation by faith plus works.

To his surprise, however, Dr. Barnhouse exclaimed, "That's exactly what the word means!" The word *believe* in the Greek is not a cheap faith, or easy believism. It is a commitment. Such is really borne out in John 3:36: "He who believes in the Son has eternal life; but he who does not obey the Son shall not see life but the wrath of God abides on him." Note how the words *believe* and *obey* are used interchangeably. The point, therefore, is to believe in Christ in such a way that your obedient will is backing up such belief. He who believes in this way shall have eternal life.

A minister was discussing electricity with an electrician. "Is it true," asked the minister, "that electricity cannot get into you unless it can get out of you?"

"That's absolutely right," answered the electrician. "Let me illustrate. When I worked in the coal mines of Pennsylvania, my brother operated one of the coal cars. I was standing on the rear of the car, singing in a carefree manner, coming to the point where the tracks divided, and my head got caught in the overhead fog. There I dangled for a moment, my feet just clearing the ground. That explains my being here today. The high voltage current could not get into me because it could not get out of me."

God's love is like electricity; it cannot get into us unless it can get out of us and share itself with others. And only a believe-obey faith will get it out of you, so that is how we must believe in Christ.

## III. Via Solid Security

Just what happens to a person who believes in Christ as the highest expression of God's love? God promises that such a person "shall not perish but have eternal life."

### *A. The Negative Aspect*

On the one hand, he will not perish. What does this mean? Its meaning is twofold: 1) "to be lost"; 2) "to perish, to suffer destruction." Which is it? Both! There need not be any ambiguity here because both meanings may be taken together, emphasizing all the more the hopeless condition of man without Christ. Such a person is on a downward trail, and the further down it goes, the worse off he gets, for he gets closer and closer to ultimate destruction, to which he is bound. In real life, perishing is not always sudden destruction. It can be and most always is a gradual process. Nevertheless, all forms of this word lead to destruction, which is the inevitable fate of all things and persons separated from God and concentrated upon themselves. There is no neutral ground between perishing and eternal life. They are absolute alternatives. But do not misunderstand: this is good news to a weary mind and a guilty conscience. Christ saves him from this. This is healing to broken bones and bleeding wounds, that Christ came not to condemn us to this perishing, but to save us from it.

### *B. The Positive Aspect*

Obviously the preferable alternative is the positive aspect of eternal life. Notice God does not say future life, but eternal life. It is the kind of life that implies not only the pardon of the convicted traitor, but also the preference, the making of him as a favorite, as his treatment in kingly honor.

Neither does God say temporal life; He says eternal life. It is a life that begins on earth the moment you believe, but because it is eternal, it lasts forever in time and eternity. It is also eternal in the sense that you can never lose it. Once you have got it, you always have it. Oh, what blessed eternal security!

If the Lord had been pleased to kill us, He would not have sent His Son among us. He came with full powers to execute judgment, which He most definitely will use upon those who do not believe. He died so that dying people in this dying world might enjoy eternal life before they die for good. This is the good news or glad tidings to a guilty conscience, to a sinner, to a person who is fed up with himself, to a person suffering in depression, loneliness, sickness, and even death that whoever believes may have eternal life. Yes, it is good news to whoever wants to start life over again, whoever wants new life, whoever wants God's life, whoever wants the breath of God, by believing in the Lord Jesus Christ. Do you believe? I hope you do, but if you do not, do so now. In the best way you know how, just trust in what Christ has done for you as the greatest expression of love.

The late Donald Grey Barnhouse and his wife went out one evening and left their children in the care of a babysitter. When they returned about midnight, the girl was greatly concerned that the oldest child had been crying for about four hours. Nothing the babysitter could do would comfort her. Dr. Barnhouse went to the child's room and found her flushed and sobbing, her face red with weeping. When he picked her up, she threw her arms around his neck and sobbed, "Daddy, say it isn't true. You do love me." He replied, "Of course, I love you." His little girl said, "The babysitter said that if I was bad, you wouldn't love me, and I know I've been bad, so maybe you don't love me."

He pressed her to himself and said, "My dear child, I always love you. When you are good, I love you with a love that makes me glad. When you are bad, I love you with a love that makes me sad. But I love you, good or bad. I am always your daddy."

The child was already calm, and the dawn of a smile came to her face. He began to cover her gently with kisses, and then he told her that a good daddy had to be with her as the Lord was with him, and with all of us who have become His children. She smiled and was soon asleep.

If you are still not fully convinced, consider this story: An English businessman visited a mission hospital for lepers in India. He was deeply impressed with the nurse's loving care of the suffering, repulsive-looking patients.

"Your humanitarian sentiment and sacrificial service for these outcasts is praiseworthy indeed," he said.

She replied, "I can assure you, sir, that if my continuance here was based only on humanitarian sentiments, I would not have the will to carry on. I would leave before nightfall. The constraining love of Christ enables me to carry on day by day."

A sad, distressed little girl told her pastor, "I want to love Jesus, but I can't do it."

The pastor said, "My dear little girl, stop thinking about your not being able to love Jesus. Just keep saying, 'Jesus loves me!' Say it to yourself many times every day."

Later the little girl returned to the pastor with a happy smile on her face. The pastor said, "I know you love Jesus. Your face tells me that you do!"

Go and do likewise!

Milton Keynes UK
Ingram Content Group UK Ltd.
UKHW010010190124
436278UK00004B/397

9 781648 951497